A BACKPACKER WHO SCRIBBLES

SOURAV SAMBIT TRIPATHY

Made with ♥ on the Notion Press Platform
www.notionpress.com

Dedicated to my Parents , My Family , Jadu sir , Abinash dada ,LFS Teachers ,LFS family ,My workout brothers, My College lecturers, College friends and the soulmates who uplifted me when i discerned a dark phase imbibing an undaunted confidence in me fabricating the writing skills with ample visionary ideas....

I AM VERY THANKFUL TO PADMASHRI HALDHAR NAG SIR FOR GUIDING ME PERSONALLY AND UPRAISING THE REGIONAL SAMBALPURI KOSHLI BHASA WHICH INSPIRES ME TO PICK MY PEN AND NOTE DOWN MY EMOTIONS INCESSANTLY...

TO EACH AND EVERYONE WHO ENJOYS THE ESSENCE OF LITREATURE DISCERNING IT..

#KALAMKAR KI SHOHRAT@2023

Contents

Contents

Contents

Contents

Contents

Contents

Foreword

TO THE UNRELENTING VOICE IN MY HEAD

THAT WILL NEVER ALLOW ME TO STOP…

#KALAMKAR KI SHOHRAT @2023

Preface

Sourav Sambit Tripathy is a 22 year old student hailing from Balangir , a small town in Odisha. His prima facie interest include composing poems, comedy and mimicry. His poetic creativity is exhibited in almost all the poems , the theme of which mainly relates to social, political , intellectual and moral renovation of human being and society. This young writer makes an incessant quest for finding out the ways and means to get back the vibrant fragrance of humanity and to retain the sanity, rationality the humankind is composed of. As a testimony to it the " A BACKPACKER WHO SCRIBBLES " aptly justify the social and human paradox testifying the maiden work as a small effort in this direction. From being a fat depressed guy of 104 kg he transformed himself facing all the criticisms and bearing the intense pain . He was not even able to run even 200 metres but he ultimately completed full marathon(42.2km) and he is fond of mountaineering and Ultra cycling (100+km). He writes when ever he feel the impulses.

The impulses generating from nature may it be forest or hill top , he inclusively binds his vision to it , to feel it, to perceive the feeling , nature wants us to understand...... By the same 22 year old author...

The book is secretly yours...

 # KALAMKAR KI SHOHRAT @2023.

Prologue

IT'S AN ORIGINAL POETRY SERIES BY MR. SOURAV SAMBIT TRIPATHY

*** " A BACKPACKER WHO SCRIBBLES " IS THE 6TH EDITION**

 # KALAMKAR KI SHOHRAT @2023.

1. INNOCENT TEARS

Crushing the financial deficit , stands a man full of drenched tears
Where heart beats just for family, least bothering himself
Where kids and wife are only option for his survival
And his heart breaks when his wife gets irritated onthe man
Leading to a solitude state of father, which others don't understand And that,
thought revolves within himself .
The man is unable to show his tears , when the girl
Still the man somehow saves a sum for his girl to seeeternal smile on her face
Deviated from his job, frustrated from the time , stillpacks a time
For his lonely wife and daughter , to make it a home.
Where even a single drop of tear from his wife and daughter makes him heartfelt
As a ship is wrecked in the violent sea , before reaching a silent shore cries for gifts,
As when the society comments him, when he purchases personal items of wife Doesn't bother him,
As the safety and sanitation of his wife and daughter ,

Is primary and at most concern , which makes him an undaunted son of a mom
Taking care of other girl as wife and making her feel alike, gives him pride
Where the pride is raised by daughter roaming freely with dad, without fear.
The sense of a word father, gets it real essence when, daughter realises,
Wife realise the great virtues of a dad, and stop irritating him at simple things
When wife starts forming a close chain of wife husband , sharing every needs
And the family runs with a swift understanding
As if a horse railing a forest Where the mind does not get stocked on what people would speak off
As a father is neglected all over, no one values theessence of tears, he shed silently
Right from birth of a daughter, to daughter getting married , is above level
The daughter and wife touches the success ,
As the one touches the sky with glory Giving the reward to the value of innocent tears .

2. THE SKY IS PINK

When I was taking a sip of tea in the adorned weather
Where the cool breeze of winds drifted my mightyhairs,
And the lovely scene made a scenic attainment in my heart
As the beauty of Himalayas is kissing its long frontiers
So was the weather tossing the uphill's of my town
Where pink blended with orange dominated the scene,
When the rain was about to cease, the chill breezestried to overlap it
The phase where mother taunted her lad to remaininside the home
Still the young prodigy, inclines to enjoy the rain , feeling the divine beauty,
Where father hides himself under an umbrella andmom enjoys it
A phase when the strong fight is faded by the strong forces of the rain
When the weather shatters the grudge of father.
The love increases along with the weather which slowly gets adorned
The feeling of romanticism casts a spell on the couple
Where understanding increases day by day, as the sun fades,

Where kid doesn't isolates himself , and a girl freely revolves all round
As the taste of kissing the soulmate , is well depicted in the happiness
Which lies on the glory of sky , fetching a sense of love in it
The craziness of me gets a boost , when my mind feels the glory
Where my friends ping me to bear mutual love , which bears a potential
Neglecting the issues , defeating the failures, solving the wrecking bomb
Doesn't take my mind to it , where it bears the hope to enjoy
As the sky is pink , my heart still yearns for blue.

3. PHASES OF GUERILLA

Mourns of pain , condolences to the bereaved family
Seems easy as when the day passes with heavy duty
Hope for family and love for land seems dauntless
Still the sword is ready to give guard of honor
And the adorned attire for the service of his land
Despite the area, despite the enemy, they show gallantry
They don't feel the peer pressure of surgical strikes
But fear for religional anarchy tenses them , breaking their mood
Tears of a wife , sadness of a mom and orphan phaseof a kid
Instill a lady to stand as an emotional pillar.
Army wife's stand as lion , as their military vermillion shoots their forehead
Giving uniform the real value it bears, which their husbands earn, by their efforts,
The love in families, the bond in troops, love for soil, is at an eternal level
A small pain in them, is pain for whole troop, but after all, a smile exerts

When a fouji enters the room, with a fearless smile and camofledge attire.

4. FEELING A SUNSET

Chirping of the cuckoo, chanting in the holy places,
revolves with all my sense
As the windy breezes trembles the tree branches making it
a scene
Where young kids come out of their four walls to ton the
ground
Where buffalos and the domesticated animals bid farewell
to crops
As the scenic essence makes it a picture instilled in many
hearts
When the grasping power of sunrays is about to fade
Mom taunts her lad to study, but he is busy in rekindling
himself
Where the taste for education and love for sports glitters,
When the man swipes his dirty sweat and return home
peacefully ,
Where mother gets ready for her husbands arrival with gift
for kids
As the Braveheart is guarding its frontiers with tasteof
sunset.

The pleasant odour of wet soil, fragrances which can fade the odonil
Where the contributions of nature, links an unending path,
Serving as a bridge between human feeling and nature
He never makes us live a solidary confined life,
Where the internal fights are summoned by low understandings
The man who make it feel the joy, the man who stay away can't,
As the wings of the bird gets energized with swift air breezes,
So as the feel of the settling sun, depicts us todays job is all done
Where our heart receives the beauty and mind scrutinizes it.

5. SHE IS A BRAVE GIRL

There lived a sister whose ideas made a link between mind and heart
Whose words of action are more powerful than just maintaining it,
Whose figure of using grammar is very strong that even I can't discern all stuffs
Where she imprints her figure on the road, and meas a small brother just follows
Where the innocent soul of mine is blessed by a non manipulated sister
Whose virtues defines her nature and a character of well being
The simple soul is much talented, whose ideas are underrated ,
As the designs of the talent can be well figured by her hold on it,
Where she don't bog down by any sort of pressure,
Where the challenging mind hunts for knowledge
She doesn't loose any temper , imparting education
And gets free to those who understand her values.

Whose words of action are more powerful than just
Bearing a beauty in heart, she is very beautiful ,isn't she ?
Where the perfect touch of kajal adorns her burkha,
And the glance of her cultural identity dominates
Still the girl, doesn't showoff, stays normal, why ?
Where the situation is well solved by the neutral piece
And her way of understanding is complete dauntless.

6. MILITARY A WAY OF LIFE

Sweet as sugar, cold as ice, hurt him once, he will thrash you thrice
Stands a youth, with full of endeavor, where the shine in his eyes
Depict the glance, where the strength of his hand combats the training
As a major is deployed to safeguard the countrymen, so as him
Whose way of speculation and an optimum deed of introspection
Is enough to make a day full of tiredness , leading tosmile in iris.
Facing the tough drill, amid the scorching sun rays ,isn't easy for minors
But he feels it, sings to it, at the hour of at most need for the troop
Where the interaction with the junior wings , is alike big brother
And the interaction with the senior wings is alike sir and cadet

Filled with enthusiasm, when he enters the parade ground, holding flag
Everyone can see the fire, both in advancing steps, and grilling commands.
Goosebumps in his hands, thousands questions in his mind with frozen toes
Butterflies in his dumb stomach is overcomed by an undaunted smile
A smile to serve the nation with valour, a smile that depicts struggle
A smile that shows the strong bonding, a smile that depicts him as a champ
March ahead my noble soldier, as the safety of our city,
Lies in your shoulders, living it by choice and letting it by chance.

7. A HIDDEN SMUGGLER

Thinking of my past , I was a proliferate dreamer lost in stories
Where my mind sailed the peaks of deomali and faint breeze
Where I was just a sole creature to spread happiness
As the virtues of the R Frost is not fulfilled without aa horse
Sailing the deep forest alike the dumb routes of mine
Achieving my rides at its own way , in an obsolete manner
Suddenly everyone's thought gets cursed by a hidden smuggler,
Whose ray of ruining people was treacherous and killing was harsh,
When the city lost its temper, demolishing the trends of abolishing it
It shook the nation, by its hampering claws , devastating the year
Where the condolences sorted to the bereaved family are almost none,

Swiping the financial efficiency of the country,
andsaddening lives
Facing the issue, where a sad farmer lost his crops by the
avenge of locust
Where the Indo china border tension, raised the level of
intrusion alarmingly
Facing the floods in Assam, where people loose their lives
defiantly
When the backbone of the country, gets shocked by soldier
getting positive
Where the entire country demands a vaccine, still the idea
is ineffective
Paving a way, for the countrymen to maintain distancing
within families
Still the Braveheart's guarding the frontiers gave a call to
the nation
Seeking , they are alive up to their last breathe , and won't
die of disease
If the situation forces them, they will go down with glory,
with a smile
A smile that energizes the countrymen to stay alert, which
influences them
Not to get thrilled by the sort of pain , the year brings
As the one who doesn't care Pakistan ,how can they get
scared of this year.

8. I CAN'T SPARE THAT LOVE

The day we leave our home , we feel we lost everything
Where a studious lady is more passionate about a profession
Where mother shed tears behind the door and father hides it
Where brother looses a friend for a period And friends starts parting,
leading their own diversified way
Still a mutual love persist hunting the real love in hometown
Mother moves to a depression when she bid adieu to her lady
And father is all about to instill a courage in mom ,facing it internally
As the lady is on the way to earn a uniform , mother dreams it ,
The day still meanders in our mind , when we think of home
When I think of parents and their struggle, I can't stop my tears

The tears which bears a struggle, the tears which would fetch glory a day.
Spending the weekend with friends in the city , doesn't give me pleasure
As my mind and heart hunts the love of parents and fight of brother
Which starts with a fight but ends with a mutual consolation,
But now , it seems a bit ignorant when , I forget tocall my parents
Engaged in some celebrations , still my heart huntsthat love
When I get ruined up in the city, I remind my mother's love
My father's affection, where I was the shining sword and they were my armor,
As the beauty of love and affection of care, seems faded in the city.

9. A LIFE YOU ARE CURIOUS ABOUT

Rejuvenation in mind , glory in vision , shine in eyes
The dauntless lady is all set to touch the sky,
Where the womanhood is upraised to eternity
Where the championship enrages the dominance As the tears of a Braveheart shields a country,
So as the lady, who shed blood so as to get adorned the best,
Clipped in the claws of the dumb , still she idolise a undaunted notion
A phase when she is torn apart, she recreates an optimum out of it
When there was noone to support , she took the shield and armour
When they was everyone , she adorned herself with cultural outfit ,
As the mighty roars of the air force jet thrills her , gives her a good feeling
A feeling which can just be felt, without any of disruption from anyone.

Some saw the dream of having a job, some made it different ,
The lady who makes a home, is guarding the frontiers,
As the love for her camo outfit adjourns her in the pavilion
Where she is the fast mirage and followers are mighty chinook,
As the river water flows within every sort of gaps ,facing adverse phase
Her minds hunts the best , and needs a life full of honour and sacrifice,
A honour of getting packed with chakras , still meanders her mind
Where the dumb driven sad phases are shattered byher undaunted smile
Where she packs her mind to be the sole self consoler of downs
Chasing the dreams, touching the barret , seems defiant for her
As the brave lady of brave parents won't get satisfied by normal dreams.

10. A CONFUSED BEGINNING

The swift breeze of air, the enhancing odor of the wind
Hooked my mind and heart in it, feeling it on its way ,
Where cool breezes of air, tilt the tree branches
And makes the leaf's fall as if , it's a way of adornment,
As when the deep essence of mind toss the scenic love
Where my nature attraction fades my phone intention
While my mind was on the raindrops , there arrived a pretty
Whose hair tossed her lohenga , and the kajal suited her look
Where I was a meandering cattle , and she was the herdsman
Where my eyes glanced her beauty, but she was unknown
The feeling of awkwardness prevailed on my face all at a sudden,
The calmness dominated the atmosphere , where I was dumb.
Few moments passed earning a unknown identity, mutually.

Where she was a desire , and I was just a flappering dolphin
When I spoke randomly on meet , my voice chocked
My eyes were shattered in her visual contact
Where she was like a burning flame and I was just a torch bearer,
When I stopped my speech , she started her wordings
Lost in the beauty , overwhelmed with internal agression
I Was a noob , where her lines were unusual for me
The day ended talking unusually , as when she approached a step ahead
Where my dreams touched the sky , and her dreams was unknown to me
Still a hope prevailed she would make it somehow.

11. I AM LEAVING PEACEFULLY

Bearing the pain isnt justified , where the near anddears taunts
Where the distress is the peak cause of ship wreckage
Where the ups isnt tolerated by some crew , who hates me
As the volcano erupts bearing a hot magma , they too hides the agony
When the soul consoler is thrashed treacherously , ruining him
So as the my life , will fade with a single blockage, ending the pain.
Everyone thinks , I must be living a funny and charming life
Who knows the pain of the sleepless nights full of depression
Where even single amount of rice can even fill my hunger
And a single nip of beer with smoke can overcome it
Still the tension dominates my mind , where I gets manipulated
Thinking I would live as myself, or shall I live like others

Being in relationship isnt a tension, neither do I bother any frustration
But my mind is unknown about the conflict, which hunts me
Where the nights are alike nomad hunting for a shelter desperately.
Quitting my life, wont just give you happiness, but also me
I will live a life full of peace, letting you to do what you can
I Won't be an obstruction in your lane.

12. ONE OF A KIND

Sweet as rasmalai, cold as black current, hurt her once,
She will break you thrice , stands as a symbol to idolise,
Her essence, clubbed with an ample amount of valour,
Where she is alike gunpowder, on her sharp rifle,
As the deep silence of forest is undone with chirpings
So as she, whose presence makes her feel the real home
Defiant by attitude , she stands as a support for inconvenience,
When the candle is about to loose it rays , by the rigorous winds,
She holds it , as a boon , to peruse her deeds shattering despondence
Where the happiness surmounts , depicting the effort of siblings,
As the tempo of the ukulele is undone without the soft fingers ,
And the tune of flute is incomplete without the pleasant vocals
Bearing all the sad phase, still she makes her best tomake other's smile
Even its a sort of dimple, or a loud laugh , she is ultimately adorable ,

When the bad times chocked her mind , she coughed it as an useless pill,
As the craze for iPhone thrills her ,so as she gets thrilled looking a starving man
Craziness to passion, thoughts to diversification,
She is alike, one of a kind, I came across .

13. MY BROTHER IS NO LESS, ALIKE MY SISTER

Depressed from setbacks , frustrated from relations , he remains dormant
Sharing every pain , caring every issue , he consoles himself silently
Relentless effort to make someone happy , doesn't upgrade him up
As he is meandering in the race , loosing his own identity,
From the depth of his emotions , he shares everything with me
But we both are dumb, instead solving , we invite dilemmas for us
The day when he stood up for me , I felt like mic got in a engine
Full of speed , full of energy , just to set a place in runaway and fly,
Where the belief and nurture is alike mom, where he gets pleasure

Remaining in daylong hunger , still he somehow arranges a meal for me
Saving money from his stipends , he makes me feelalike his girlfriend
Where evn a single smile in my face , make him feel the brave lad he is
When there was no one to bear my pain, he came as boon
Where the minute understandings prevails and shatters a dark phase
As the lonely devotee is on its way to kedarnath , so as he ,
Who bears a bullet to my arms , and an outfit for my camo,
Whose way to things right, is well versed with my mind-set,
As the only soul hunts him , where there's no one to beat around my bush
Seems as a father figure in care , does a mother rolein cooking,
He is just adorned with everything , the eternity dominates the scene.

14. AN UNTOLD PAIN

Defeating the phase of intense pain in periods ,
Stands a girl with an undaunted mindset,
Where the abrupt thoughts dominates her mind ,
Still the low minded brain defeats the pressure
Things change when , she gets taunted , ignoring it
Thinking as if it's a curse for a girl child
A place where the country declared , equality in status
The girl doesn't get the real status , as it remains hidden,
An instance where someone understands her , shefeels good
Paving a way for affection , as she lies freckle all over ,
Where her mind gets an intense conflict relating it with others
As a mom who makes a family, faces the same
Abruptness in menstrual cycle, dumbness in mind
Innocence in heart , pain in body and mind
Doesn't make the scene beautiful , but she tries it
Where good behavior uplifts her sad mind .
And make her feel , its natural all over the phase
Still the question remains , why do girls suffer this ?
As the water crushes the dam and paves its way ,
She crushes the pain and move in her own way

Where the dauntless angel degrades the old minded thoughts,
Letting it a way to think same , as all mothers face it
From puberty to the menopause , the story remains same,
The story where the greatness of a girl cant be depicted .

15. WE CAN'T DEPICT IT IN ROLLS

If you are a shining sword , I am your shield,
If you are a swift breeze , I am a typhoon,
If you are a lady full of determination , I am a manfull of emotion,
Where my mind hunts you , and your mind hunts for love
The love , which is not indistinct, the love which is deep rooted ,
Where the passion is about to dominate the climate of togetherness.
The interrogative narration created by me , is well spiced by you,
Where each day all starts with a craziness , and ends with a funny fight
The fight which involves no one, the fight which don't involves any rings,
The calmness prevails , when I imagine you , feel the essence of yours
Where a lady is desperately struggling to achieve success , with a hope

A hope which surmounts a small part of mine in her
rigorous journey .
The life gets a deep essence of solitude , when she , doesn't
call me overnight
When the root cause of her depression is her compassion
for career,
As the plane is about to take-off on time , least bothering
the passengers
Where her mind tends to love the education , neglecting
what commoners say,
She increases her understanding capacity , so as to tune to
me
On my songs , and help me over my daily life dilemmas .
Passing the awful days, enjoying the naughty moments ,
meanders in me
Where I made someone smile , where I made a girlto
improve her levels
Where she got upraised from a miniature to a passionate
girl
The livelihood of the moments cant be just depicted
scrolling her pics
Where we bear a love which doesn't lie on objects , neither
on beauty
Does only lie in the passionate maturity we bears , where
eternity dominates.

16. LIVING BY CHOICE

Moving of the legs on a rhythm when my ears hears the pleasant beats,
Moving of the neck making a tone , when no one is near you,
Moving of toes on a ground , when no one watching you,
Moving of hands with a brush, when you visualizea scene,
Is that not a passion , which evokes when no one is with you,
When you faced a crushing defeat , but it stands , decreasing pain
As when the ship is about to depart a shore , so as the passion,
When the world forces the kid to choose a job, despite his interests
Where the essence of taste is taken from him , like a dumb driven fellow
When the lion is forced to live in water , where hisimportance sheds,
As a boy is forced to follow the decision , which is trending in the culture

Where the importance of money is more than the humanitarian virtues
Life is unique , but the lad is confused on himself of accepting or retarding
Where the emotions of parents is more for him ,neglecting the way of life
And the conflicting scenes of cars and life partner make him tense
Prone to drugs or the loss in emotion , takes away his love for himself
Where he is lost to find himself, the way of him , the style seems meaningless
As the man is paid salary without the meaning of job he is perusing
Its uncertain where the love fades, where the gust to discover himself ceases
Where the life throws a lot of setback , where he is emotionally blackmailed
The kid who follow it , remains as a trend , but theother knows himself
Where he would draw a channel and dig a tunnel to reach the shore
Where the love for passion doesn't eradicates , as an angel is bond to a prince.

17. DAUNTLESS LAD

From the dusty storms , to fierce winds , stands
theendeavor of a man in camofledge
On the strands of chicken corridor to the encroaching Thar
desert
The defiant boy seems fearless rising the tricolour
Where mind gets diversified in raising the respect for attire
and
His body gets tested upto an optimum level.
Sailing the forest , wearing an outfit seems easy for him
As the fighter boy is highly nurtured by the love of soil
Where he waits for a letter from home ,
Exhausted from service , impressed from the odor of the
wet soil
Doesn't let the brave soldier gets depressed in any
condition
Underestimated military personnel stands as idol , as
when
The strength of a personnel is energized, where the
condolences
Provided to a bereaved family is upraised,
As the son lies in hand of holy mom , as the tears can't
depict the pain

And flashes on the homecoming of the dauntless warrior.

18. KARGIL VIJAY DIWAS

Beautiful as it seems , kills many hours of undaunted dreams,
Where the best of best gets faded , but a few , just gets it
Adorned with the uniform , stripped by emblem , stand defiant
Where the footsteps of them measures the height of the Himalayas
As the kid gets nourtured by his mom , sleeping calmly in her arms
They work for the mother , to prove they are sons , full of capabilities
Family get in tears , when he bids adieu , to serve for the kargil war
Where her mom makes him adorned with her immense blessings
And father makes his heart defiant , as his soul is ready to serve country
The long war takes up lives , demolishing the trends , which we all follow

The trends of sleeping , the types of food , the calmly in her arms instinct to waste time
He stands , making a promise , he will hang the flag at the hilltop
The colour of blood they shed , show a dauntless emergence of valour
Where there is a promise of a mother , a risk of vermilion of a wife
The reputation of a father and the sacrifice of a kid, that cant be depicted
Listening to the beauty of the anthem , he sets himself fearless,
Either to die , or to kill the enemy , who try to occupy our motherland
The story doesn't gets an ending , as a soldier always remains a soldier
If the countrymen think , martyrs memories are lost in the war ,
What is the kargil war memorial , where the engravings are glorious
Where the attire , adorned with a cap and a gun , with a folded flag
Makes a scene , which brings tears to the one who think he's patriotic
As the glorious effort of soldier cant be felt by many , busy in the work

Still the burning MASHAL , shows the gallantry pride of the innocent blood .

19. A KINSPERSON

Within the deepness of sorrow, she exerts a dauntless smile
From the glowing eyes to soorma , she just stares
From the prudent burkha , she shows her culture
Depicting the depth of friendship , she shows her secularism
Modern thoughts , diversified mindset seems beautiful
Beauty in heart , beauty in mind seems prolific
The openness in way and upwelling from inside
Seems as if a sister is a lone mate of a brother
Where she extends mutual collaboration to share secrets
Depicting the unity amid all the ups and downs
In every instance of the phase , I promise you
You might shed tears , but I can't wipe it out
You may feel the pain, but I wont be there to comfort you
But still , a hope exist where the homecoming , thrashes all pain.

20. HAPPY RAKSHYA BANDHAN

From the humiliating days to the brightest moments,
Her behavior doesn't change , she remains the same
Where the simplicity clubbed with emotion is adorable
Where the law of understanding is more than gifts
As a father , let his son feel his efforts , so as she
Who doesn't want the presents , just want an attention
The odd dumb days , where I fetched no improvement
She stood near me , instilling a ray of hope inside me
When my family and my cousins are afraid of my problems
She makes a genuine approach, to know and clear my issues
When the food was about to get distributed , she gave her part
The love which has no frontiers, still the hunt for Cadbury dominates
Waiting for me , long days , to tie a rakhi , is just for me
But she ties her emotion within it , bearing a sadness in face
So as I am about to bid adieu , for my hectic job , leaving her

Still the friendly mind , paves a goodbye , hiding her tears
Where each drop of tears bears , a role in adorningmy upbringing
The upbringing which increases the essence of mybeautiful attire
Finally , it leaves a smile in my face , when I remember those fighting days
The memories that fades away , still she bears the same emotion for me .

21. CORONA A PATHFINDER FOR MONEY PLUNDERERS

Beating the financial crisis ,stands the farmers demanding for their payment
Defeating the border tensions , stands the undaunted troops of Indian army
As the way to live a living , is just by making others feel safe , despite their family
Where the widow of a jawan cries , making his kids feel , how great their father was
Where the old farmer dies facing a crisis of crop failure and manipulation in wages
Still the mighty innocent hearts thrives for a ordinary living , accompanied by food
Where the government send funds , for the warriors , the corrupts dislocates the fund
Leading a way for money laundering , where the subordinates brutally disrupts it

With no accountability , each and every person , gets thrashed , who enquires it
As the doctor saves life of a patient least bothering his family , so as a worker
Whose code of conduct , gets hidden , highlighting the ways the big official follows ,
Where the autocracy purchases the media personnel's , with a good sum
The phase where the poor shed their tears , facing the corona count in country
The police man gets equipped with a heavy workload , running day and night
Least bothering the subordinates who have a cleanchit in disrupting the count
Where the pain and agony of innocence is least bothered by the money plunders
Whose way of speculation is cheap , whose way oflooting money is at optimum
As the media is just for showing the narcotics bureau , and the Rhea case
The manipulated media , is under the godfathers ofthe industry , who feeds them
Where the decreasing gdp is not important as the ylevel security of Kananga
Where the border tension is not as important as the justice for Sushant

Hiding the real terrors of the country who are partly responsible for all cases .

22. DAUNTLESS WOMAN

If I am just a sound of letter , she is a sentence
If I am just a boy full of grief , she is a river full of emotions
If I know how to create a wound, she know how to heal it
Where the drops of blessing get showered from her virtues
Where her head is full of defiance aiming to make Home
The gist of ocean isn't shattered by the waves splashing the shore.
Mother by duty and wife by husband strength, makes her adorable
Where the innocence prevails upon the fierce attack of father
And the interrogative mind of a lad , dreaming something
The craze of the glorifying vision takes up the heart to eternity
Where the service is summoned , and she is on her way.
Heading a mission towards a effective visualisation
Disrupted from heart , broken from neighbours
Fainted from the work , shattered from the belief
Still she gets the courage to hold the hope of a family

Where the weird answer rejuvenates the priority
Leading a way to a self instilled love and care for oneself
Where the love starts from feeding a baby and making him sleep
I am lost in the thought of girls having an inner strength, the eternal one
Which is not faded by the emotional storms , not shattered by the breakups
Heading a goal , as if a lion is in charge of his kingdom.

23. STOP NEPOTISM

I don't know when will I rise , it hurts me , it chokes me
Where the aristocratic legacy surmounts the scene,
Taking it a way to identify the real skills , remains ignorant
As the archer shoots an arrow , without looking itssides ,
So as the royal people launches their dumb kids , neglecting many,
Where the depression of a innocent lad , forces him to commit suicide
Those cruel eyes couldn't see the pain of a father saving money ,
To send money to his struggling kid , the pain of amother ,
Who hides her tears behind the door , when she bids adieu,
The pain of a friend when he miss his soul , still the thought hunts
He has gone to make us proud , least bothering thestruggle they bear
But the innocence is ruined by some sort of ruthless
persons , who adds fame to their stock of recognitions.
Deviated by mind , frustrated from the dumbness ,neglecting virtues

He thinks why for he choose this line as a career ,full of nepotism
Where the best of best gets rejected at a single shot,
But the worst talents easily gets notified by their worthy fathers
Where care and emotions of the parents isn't concerned
As the so called legacy prevails in every field of line .

24. I WILL BE A PART OF YOUR HOMEMAKING

Frustrated from the work load , depressed from thepassing time,

My eyes glance a pain in your eyes , which you hide it by smiling

The pain which deviates your mind , the pain which squeezes your energy,

Still you try the best , to make our home , and takecare of me and kid ,

Doing it tirelessly , makes you realize , my husband is enjoying his day ,

But who knows , the part which you leave behind , is accomplished by me

I don't Feel the real pain , as you bear , but I try to understand it ,

The phase when you return home , turn to bed without dinner ,

The instance where you don't spare a time for yourself , still give time to kid,

The wrong notion which I bear , is well eradicatedby your efficient work
The source of yours which don't let me to stress my mind in household works
Still I try , to be a part of yours , finishing the work ,you leave undone
I get tears in my eyes when I see my wife in pain, and I have nothing to do
Except talking her , pressing her head , and leaving her sleep peacefully
Where the stress is more than enjoying , where the rest is the real happiness
When her body rests and I just take my seat near her legs , and press it gently
To make her feel , her husband does care for her , when she is in pain
But the naughty mindset of her listen to my sad words , and makes fun of me
She is no less a best friend to me , who understands me the most , to share everything
From choosing a saree to preparing a meal , she respects my opinion,
Where the bonding is much more than buying expensive gifts for one another ,
Where the day culminates with a pinch of happiness, and a lot of fun against me

Because I love to see her smile , which packs my mind to do more of my work
As , I Earn for my family , for their smile , I am ready to spare my time and affection .

25. MY MIND STILL HUNTS YOU

Peeping into the recycle list , I found a pic of yours,
Where your hairs cast a bliss , making your face pretty
Where your eyes , tossed the glamour of kajal,
Where the long nose of yours , made it a speculated sarcasm,
Where the color of your lips , tossed the rigor in it ,
And the pretty smile , that made my day blissful , many a times
It has been so long , where I haven't taken you in my arms ,
Where the sort of my high temper , just get cools down easily
As the fish is used for bait , so as the innocence is used, to make happy,
Those days , where the narrative spell was dominant all over ,
When the flock of flowers , is adorned in your hairs , as if its portrayed
Still the innocence in your heart kills my agony ina simple way
I Bow down, when your face appears in my mind

The softness in you , the charming smile in you,
Just pass as a memory down the dusty lane ,
Where your priceless emotion doesn't gets easily faded ,
When I feel it , I cant stop my tears , my hearts gets overwhelmed
Still we need to move , eradicating the darks ,
andcherishing the togetherness
we have been through, these years.

26. SISTER WHOSE SMILE DOMINATES THE SCENE

Defeating every odds of the dumb society, stands an angel,
With an undaunted belief, kissing the glory at her frontiers,
Where the blessing of Diversed mind condolise thebad phase
As a plane is ready for take off amid the weather, so as she
The girl who is ready to achieve her compassion, with a passion
And a well equipped vision in her eyes, which shines everyday
A phase where the everyone betrays, her own companion consoles her
Leaving the family, studying abroad, makes her sad at many instance
But her dumb comic mind anyways recreates a scene in it,
Where friends are about to bid adieu, she can't stop her tears shedding

Somehow her broad smile relentlessly tries to hide it and bid a farewell
The story where she is a shining armour , and her family is her sword
The mind which taste I phone, and the craze of tiktok,
Can't dominate her mind , a mind full of diversified outlook
A heart which has guts to bear pain, an eyelid which has power to hide tears,
Makes her an efficient lady , as the lion grudgeshatters a dog bark
She shatters everyone who thinks she's incapable and weak ,
As the vision of making it , with her way , makes her unique .

27. BABU SHONA TRENDS

Starring at those tears of a mother who doesn't get money
to feed her kids
Looking in the eyes of a father who gets ruined bythe lavish
marriage expense
Feeling the hardship of a brother who serve the frontiers ,
to earn a living
Listening to the radio , where the Assam flood victims , die
of negligence,
Smelling the shirt of a street peddler , whose poverty hunts
him daily
Visioning in the hard lips of a saliva licking kid who takes
sleep under a bridge.
Still I am confused , as the one who was once a girl
wanderer , gets changed
When the story of a struggling kid ruining his love
attraction and all desires
Hunt for attire and desperately tries to be in list of the
Indian martyrs
Where the smell of land matters , where the love ofparents
matters

Where the uniform as camo matters , where the cool breeze matters
Least bothering the babu shona culture which the youth follows.
He stares at the settling sun , and gets a deep essential vibes of love
His mind searches for the love of a girl , still he isntready to cheat her
As living a life full of emotion is not expensive as living a life less ordinary
Whose strong touch of the hand neutralise the burden in many ways
Whose nerves and the foot condition shows the love for his duty
As the wordings and the love of a commander is much loyal to him
I know the one who serves the frontiers , returns home after a long gap
Still the actual love isnt faded , where the one who gets loved awaits
Behind the door and just pray for his goodness , degrading the upliftment
Where the trueness is beyond the babu shona , and the trust is above baby.

28. FEMALE FOETICIDE

Blessings cast a spell , where a man heard of his wife , getting pregnant
When the measures of ultrasound report suggest a baby in her womb
The mother gets , a pleasure and justify a month tohold his baby on her arms
Splashing against the walls of wormhole, kicking the surface of her belly
Doesn't Seems weird , but when the next check is done after months
To check the baby sex, proves fatal for a mother and the child
The process of hatred starts , when the sex is disclosed as a baby girl
Seeming a burden for his family , where the man listens to his family
Neglecting the nurturing of wife and her pregnancy
Taunting her ,
Torturing her seems easy for him, As his aim is to kill girl

Who doesn't increase the number of family members , Lest destroys the money
From her feeding to expenses in her marriage.
'Is sex done in hope of a boy', the question revolves
Where a mother is about to shatter , without the support of husband
Where her own father , with the consent of others Is about to kill his daughter
This thought creates a hatred among the family , where the mother just cries
And she is lost in the thought , to flee from house or to do this offence
In killing an innocent tiny , in her worm
Dejected from thoughts , fear from family , no support of husband
Makes her cry at every single state , where she isn't capable of herself
Sharing it with own parents is even harmful as her mother wants a male heir
The family should be aware, that the dynasty being ruled by a father Is itself created by a MOTHER who is a GIRL .

29. TO ALL MY BHAIJANS

Paving a way to holy kabba isnt difficult for a man with pure laws ,
Where the beards give a touch to the holy hat , making him bhaijan
Where the eagerly emotions awaits for the bhaijan to complete his Nawaz
Where the beauty and the culture is well portrayed in their systems
Where the affection lies in a man , to secure the faith and follows his rules
As an officer is deployed to save his territory from goons
Where the fierce lad gives the security to all girls of the country undauntly
Least bothering the visuals and media he keeps on helping without expectation
Making a way to a well defined secularism , where the work toss the beauty
And the innocence touches the bravery, as when it is needed

The friendship is as deep as a treasure , and as strong as thread rakhi band
Where the brutality of the false leaders are shattered by the friendship
As when one hear " Allah ho Akbar" that reminds us of the preaching of Allah
Where the self flagellation and circumcision seems easy for the brave lads
As the pain and struggle is for them , seems as a defiant blessing
Where the burkha and holy kajal makes a girl adorable , as a tale of Portia
As she revolves around the streets , thinking there are brothers to save her..
Making it a sense of abundance of a great cultural overview
The secularism which they show is humanitarian , the love they show is eternal
The tears which they shed is blissful , the character they show is benevolent ,
The speech they use is sweet , the attire they wear is adorable
Where the depth of bond show the diversity in unity and bonding is attractive in one's vision.

30. MY OWN BROTHER

Amidst the emotional challenges , he's the one to stand as a shield
From the worst academic surprises to best results, he doesn't leaves me alone
Standing behind me at every empowerment fronts , and walking in front
As if a lion is deployed to save his countrymen , he protects me.
Fulfilling the wish as he could , lending me some penny to buy chocolates
He doesn't share it , as sisters happiness is more than saving money for stuffs
Eradicating a scene where , I am betrayed , he secures me at every instinct
Taking me to have a cup of coffee and have a handful of chocolates ,
He understands how to heal a shattered phase of mine
Making me a way long to motivate , to understandthe values of parents

Where he gave a Handbag of dress , when I wanted just one
Where he made me feel he's the one , when I had no one to listen
Parents made me feel , I am the odd one , taunted me at every now and then,
He hold me at his arms , swiped my tears and encouraged to move ahead
When I thought of getting a dumb brother, he evoke as a resilient one
Paving a far flung in his studies to making me feel I had my own duty,
He never returns back, unless I do a job with discipline,
And refreshes my mind at a miniature effort
Chocolates doesn't matter , neither do a bunch of dresses matter ,
Only thing which joins me , isnt portrayed in any thing , of what I can't
He thinks of me ,being a child , matters the most
Remaining hungry , when I am sad , Cancelling his match , when I am caught .

31. VOICE OF A COMMONER

Paving a deep sleep , where my dreams tossed the grains of epitome
Where the ideas of the teaching is beyond the optimum thoughts
Where the perfection was evenly distributed among all scholars
As the rich laden workloads was meant for firm dedicated stuffs
Where the overnight howling and the day-long gossip , touched the eternity
As the companion for the suffering ,were a defiant troop of dauntless lads
All at a sudden , my overlong dream took a tough break , where mind got still
Deviated in the pandemic , the whole era is suffering , like dumb driven creatures
Where the income is below the level to feed a stomach , where the price hikes are more
Where the burkha is replaced by N95 masks , as the decorated masks are for fashion

Days where the kids , glanced the beauty of outdoor sports
, got stocked in virtual games
Days where the old age groups , shared their happiness in
parks , is screwed away with closure
Days where the fitness freaks , reached the gyms before
time , got thrashed by the lockdown
Days where the media hunts the ncb , the gdp of country
degraded at a sharp rate
As the happiness of work doesn't lie in accomplishment ,
just lies in the present attendance list
Where the productive youth , gets Frustrated by the closure
of mood , inside the four walls
India needs a scrutiny where the deeds of youth gets
recognized amid all the setbacks
Where the firm education is well guided and provided to
each and every student in villages
Where the opening of the parks with proper medication is
useful , to boost their moods
Where the youth gets a home duty , despite the urge for
rigorous attendance hunting's
We need a life full of excitement and enthusiasm , despite
the odd system of sprouted minds .

32. MY MIND HUNTS THE WISE DAYS

Day I realized , we were brought up in the same manner,
Where the innocent heart is Unknown about the betray,
When the mind is compressed by the family tensions,
The day where the fight starts with the grudge of father
But ends with the deep crying of mom , shedding tears behind door
Where parents fought all over , but my mind was unknown
Frustrated from the educational failures, irritated from the family members
The heart is shattered , when no one helps to console me ,
When we faced a phase , where there was nothing left ,
To the phase where I thought I was almost all done,
When I faced failures , I peeped at my footsteps that I had,
Where I bear a place in my parents heart, still getting neglected
My heart gets in a phase of deep solitude, when I get no one to share
Where my heart just thumps, and feel sadness , knowing it would end

I don't know how my mother faced it , from these long years,
Without getting support from anyone , but being everyone's victim
I know it would end soon, and we can restart a new phase happily
Still my mind hunts , the day , where I will fetch a love an eternal one .

33. I FEEL SOMETHING AROUND YOU

The sun is about to shade, and I have a thought of rejuvenation
The mind where my thoughts revolves on him ,
Where the dumbness of mine is uplifted and encouraged
Until it makes a short crisis , involving him , making a memory
The phase where we both have an instilled precision of defining love
Where it starts with KAISE HO and end with AACHE SE KHANA KHA KE SONA
I think of me , am I a person eligible for him , he thinks the same
The bond where there are fabricated lies, but he wont start the day with a lie,
The sphere which I need, is well provided , as if an asteroid is chasing earth
Where the justification is not required for him , where I delay my regularity

The peace which I need, is not understood by many , but he defines me
The solitude which I need out of peer pressure is well consoled by him.
The glory in his eyes , hunting for his dream , doesn't get shattered
When I entered his life , neither he did any realization
Helping me from solving those question to making me feel energized
He always makes me feel , he's a brave lad of a brave mom
Where the scrutiny and the defiant heart is well perceived for me
When I was about to choose the stars , he made it shine like scorching sun
Our love doesn't lie in the text , or do exist in the messages
Our love lie in the way he makes me feel what I am, and what I need
Either it may be a bit of dairy milk or a Barron of Indian Navy ,
He makes me feel the real version of me , the real potential which I bear.

34. I KNOW WHY I AM SAD

The day I realised , we were brought up in a same manner,
Where the innocent heart is unknown about the betray,
When the mind got depressed , having a look on family tension
The day where the fight starts on the financial crisis , with no help
And ends up self realising , shedding tears behind the doors,
Where parents knew all , but our curative mind was unknown
Frustrated from the educational backs, irritated from the homely tensions
The lady is deepening her thoughts , visioning the cruelness of the society
Where we faced a phase , where there was none toswipe our tears,
But there was many to push us to depression , and enjoy that pain
When I got failures , I turned to steps, realising that I was something

Where I bear a part in my parents heart , still getting neglected
My heart gets a deep solitude, when I get no one toshare my depression
Where my heart just thumps , and feel the sadness ,knowing it would end
I don't know , why my eyes see my mother in your eyes , bearing the same
The pain which is not consoled by anyone , but is hurt by everyone
The pain which needs no alarm to arrive , the painwhich is above all,
I know it would end with the passage of time , andstill the hope of good days
Are yet to arrive in the pleasant shore.

35. YOU ARE A REASON TO FALL IN LOVE WITH

Frustrated from my work schedule , hunting for someone to bother ,
I just remind your good virtues , being the toughest to being silliest
You have a different perspective to work on different aspects ,
May it be playing with my cousin's , or handling your tight workload
You leave a footprint for me , to walk on , following the mild steps
The steps of innocence , the prints of self belief through this journey
When the self mind deviates me from my goal , you help me to realize it
When I get stuck in bitter hardships , you form a chain of motivation around me
Where the mind is about to take a deep nap , my heart still hunts your face

As the castle is incomplete without a handful of sand , so as you
Whose ways of helping never ends , lest it faces a sharp inclination ,
As the love for each other , strengthens with the passage of time with each other
You are a reason to fall in love with , as the one who is busy in her own work
As the one who dreams big , gets connected to my self emotions , easily
The one whom I can share my opinions and matters , with much ease
As the one who understands me and values me , from depth of her soul
Possibly gets a good connection , least bothering the weather conditions
The weather of depression , the weather of frustration , the weather of getting cheated.

36. COME TO AND ADORN MY ATTIRE

How can I describe you , whose spirit is undaunted
Whose love is above domestic walls , whose
Behavior is reassuring and whose beauty is prolific
Cumulated within the society ,but has a different way of living
The process which is not embarked , the space
Which is not investigated , letting her to enjoy herself
Her stepping into home with glorious eyes
She guards herself as an queen taking over royal treasury
As she is adorned with a gift , as a boon is overhead
Where the stars inclines and changes , after she stares
And the beauty of sunset is above all dilemmas.
Brightness in eyes , adornment in beauty
Dauntless in courage , skilled in education
Seems a loving atmosphere, when both virtues matches
When I cries for her love , and she understands the pain
Where I tackle the problem and she reviews it
It's a journey from the dusty streets of Balangir .

37. BHAGBAN HAI KAHAN RE TU

Thinking about a new idea to confess a girl , I chant your name
Taking dip in the river water to meditating in home , I remember you
Waking up in early morning to ending my day peacefully , I fold my hands
Helping a poor to arguing a spendthrift , I suggest your way of eternity
As a son is meaningless , without the care of mother, so as you
Every work seem difficult , where your blessings are not overhead
But as the passing days , and the emotional attachment with you
I feel my link is fading day to day , where the sole is suffering
A suffering , where a friend lost his parents , wherea shop ,
Gets washed away by floods , where the blast shatters the panels

Where the money doesn't reaches the poor , and the world gets trauma
A pain which every family bears , and hopes a blissful blessing of yours
When the politics starts with your name , spreadingthe hatred on humanity
As the disease is overloaded ignoring the infected blood we bear
Where the society gets separated on basis of hierarchal order of precedence
Where the soldiers gets blamed for border tensions , amid the regional disputes
The mountain which seemed sacred , is now a business epicenter of looting,
As often poor gets cheated in your name , and gets ruined easily
You can come to me with helping mindset , where the land is not ignored
Where the teary eyes of every single being , is well felt by your grace
You can turn for me and leave me in ghastly desert of immense despair
But you need to provide smile to a bereaved family with full condolences
And a will power to resist the upcoming hardship , the hardship of money
The hardship of marriage , the hardship of education.

38. STILL THE QUESTION ARISES, WHO IS SHE

Hitting the clock , jogging at a sway , I was busy at my balcony,
The thunder was striking the ears , and the drops were lashing ,
The drop made the soil smell a effective odor , pleasant to smell
Meanwhile , I saw a girl from my balcony , adorned with a red top
Whose sandals tossed the ground with less sound
Where the optimum visuals were making me feel alive
Her hair were long , black coloured with a pinch of mehendi
As if a shower of waterfall is covering the rigid mountain walls Her eyes were faint black ,
Adorned with kajal on her lids Making her touch sense the way , I want to feel
Her face was less powered , with a glassy view of pimples
And her neck was glorified with a sparkling necklace .

The down trodden girl seemed a piece for joy for me at an instinct
Where my eye peeped the mole beneath her mouth ,
As i was the one desperate for her homecoming , chilling at her sway
I met her at once , and the perpetual look of her glanced all way
Where the stuffs of the phones seems least bothering for her ,
Busy in conversation , the sun was about to shed down.

39. THE INNOCENT HEART

From the darkest days , to the brightest nights
She makes me feel she is the one , consoling me Every phase
,
Every moment , any circumstance, She held my hands ,
and
Eat whatever I give her , the tears in her eyes , the beauty
in her hairs
The innocence in her soul , the rudeness in her bark,
bridges me
When I mourned , she gave me the happiness,
When I enjoyed , she was active part in celebration,
When I got choked of my duty , she gave her time
As the sailor is commissioned for a ship in high tide ,
Where the daylong frustration ends with her commitment
A Person can hurt my sentiments , but she wont ,
As the love increases everyday with the time, Fading all
bad memories and instilling good actions
Where my cause of solitude is well understood by her As
she deserves a love alike a maternal care ,

Where I am her mom and she is my daughter, who rules my heart and makes the human I am.

40. WHEN THERE WAS NONE, SHE HELD MY HAND

From dawn to dusk , her blessings made my day ideal
Where a prodigal brother as me is transformed into a loyal one
Where a sister shade is very essential for my improvement
As the commander who guides a commodore , so as she
When I got detached from my studies , she was the fiercest
When I got attached to my passion hunting my dream , she was the coolest
When the family cousins betrayed me, she stood as a barrier for me
Where there was a game with my emotions , she upraised it
Where the whole family cousins were egoistic , she was the most humble
As the boon is blessed by god , her blessing makes me feel alive
When the education waits my mind fetch it.
She makes a way for a specific mission with an Authentic vision

The society says, if there is no blood link , there is no relation
But the big sister makes me feel , we are born to same mom
Where I was the dumb , and she was the coolest of all,
Where I was the troop , and she was the officer ,
As the dumb brother is saved from drowning by her virtues
Where she was the stars in the sky , and I was blessed with her glory.

41. LET'S BEGIN IT AGAIN

Scrolling the texts , searching our pics in laptop,
Seems our relation is fainted , but the memory isn't
The realization which I bear now , is of no use
When you got agitated because of my dumb actions
Where I was a faint person and you were a light in my life
As when we both moved apart , now it seems a bit awkward to speak to you
My mind still hunts the day , when we spent time together
From the chai wale to golpappa shots, your smile was my motivation,
When you laughed , I got excited to make nuisanceactivities ,
When you cried , I realized my fault in it and tried to heal it
Though it was tough for me to understand you , still trial was my passion
To explore you to your best version of yours, to chill happily
Now ,it has been 3 yrs, we got no connection,
When my bitter truth was unbearable for you,

When you stood , to love me , knowing I was a dumb prodigal,
As I couldn't satisfy your good virtues , I feel I am offended internally
Where my heart beats for your pain and meanders on my mistakes
Though we are separated , still I am ready to accept you ,
As the 1st meet we had in our collage ,my heart cries Lets begin it again, lets begin it again.

42. A SISTER IS BEHIND ME

Beating the gust of spine chilling cold in the dawn ,
To abrupt heat in the dusk , she remains undaunted,
Where the lonely soul desperately hunts the perfection
As the chirpings of the birds cast a narrative spell onnature,
So as she , whose wise nature of living , steals the show ,
But the innocent mind , sings to me , in hour of atmost need
Betrayed from family , depressed from educational setbacks
She stands stills , when I share my cause to the failure ,
Guiding me , narrating the examples of how I was , she never leaves me
Taunting me at my faults , praising me on my struggles ,
She never makes me feel , she is sister to other blood
Where the stars in the brothers attire is at peak of her priority
She is a boon for me , whose blessing shatters my despondence
Whose shower of consoling words , makes a day charming,

Whose belief in me , make me feel the defence lad, I am
Where the society is busy chasing the same , she is different
Whose taste of kissing the dream is awkward for others ,
Restricting what others speak , she doesn't get
manipulated.

43. HAPPY FRIENDSHIP DAY

Sharing my moments of ample joy to bitter grief , he is there behind me
Where my mind desperately searches for him , when the trauma is overhead
As the mig 21 is incomplete without a firm wing commander , so as he
Who doesn't let me feel the one in sorrow , or neither make me feel I am lonely
When the mutual interaction is sufficient to solve any issue , either of academics
Or of the phase we all go through, the state where the solitude dominates,
The instance when the packed up government gave a huge blow , he laughed at it
Where the difficulty level of questions was at peak , he solved it with a smile
Where the current broke up , he gave a expressionfull of joy , hiding his tears
When the closest of his troop , doesn't bothered him , he just reminds me

The friendship which doesn't depends on someone, to prove an ecstasy .
The ecstasy which shows the broad smile , bearing the the broken soul relied on others
Proving it with lines , or giving a touch posting a video won't suffice,
As the moments , where both cried , and the joy which we fetched near the pond
Seems an emotion which we can't fetch in this hectic schedule , still we try
The bond where the third person , isn't allowed to control the efficiency
Neither of a silky joy or a beautiful piece , the emotions is more than a relationship
Where the eternal bond touch the sky with glory, ejecting a roar amid the climate.

44. STRUGGLE WORTH REMEMBERING

From the thrilling 3 AM cycle ride to paddling 100 km with josh
From the exhausting 250 m run to finishing a full marathon ,
From getting mentally exhausted to summiting thehill top ,
It wasn't easy , nor was a task for faint hearted
Whose eyes just glanced working least bothering perfection
Where the mobility controlled by mental stability is well concerned
Days where my body pain was about to dominate my stability
Where my crushed thighs , rotten fingers and scorched face ,
Were all set to fret my daily schedule , amidst the activities
But the mind was all set to perform all with mental ease
As the Gurkhas are bound to take care of their kukri dagger

So as I , whose aim was to complete a gruelling work with smile
Traveling over thousand miles , running over hundred miles ,
Gave a motivation where Self respect dominates the whole scene
Where need of even a friend with a bottle of water seems important
As working on the devised plan differentiates you from the mediocre crowd
Who are always to criticize you on various conflicts you encounter.

45. HAPPY REPUBLIC DAY

Sweet as mother , cold as father , hurt him once , he will kill you forever
Stands the brave warriors of Indian forces amidst the regional blows
Defeating the intense cold of the leh ladakh , and the heat of thar ,
From the slump area of sundarbans to the optimumends of kanyakumari,
He stand dauntless , facing the criticism , but the brave heart is emotional
May it be Facing the stone pelting or the inter regional disputes
Bidding adieu to his crying family , this young handlebar moustache fouji
Leaves his station , suppressing his emotion , he thinks of the nation
Where the safety of nation in frontiers is more preferred than his family ,
He takes the oath of serving the land with valour and wisdom promoting surakshya

When the nation was in need of protection , they called our soldiers from ends,
But when it is the moment of success, the bereaved politicians takes their place.
Paving a good bye to his life , he remains defiant , where his hands beckons the moustache
Where the glory of eyes is enough to kill the courage of enemy defeating their strength,
He repeats the statement , " tell my mom , not to cry , as his son gave his life for nation,
Tell my wife , that his husband lied down looking her picture in wallet ,
Tell my son , that everything I bear will be his , from dms shoes to military jacket
Tell my brother and sister , my keys of my Enfield will be permanently theirs"
Celebrating the republic day , without understanding the values of sacrifices is meaningless
Understanding the deeds of theirs , with love for service to others is high yielding
Lets unite the hands , lets unite the vision , lets unite all races and all religions
To lead a life free of narrow domestic wall , where the glance of eyes will bear balidan
Where the sacrifices of a family wont suffer , and the bondage of army troops will remain same.

46. MY PARTNER

Loving you from dawn, till dusk signifies your presence
Where your beauty doesn't just recline in external mien,
But it equips an eternal site in my feeble heart ,
Where I play the role of a cracksman, but you are still same,
As the monsoon tent requires its porch to form a complete unit
So as I, who needs you in our ups and downs , facing together
When there was none ,to listen my frustrations , she listened calmly
When there were just few to motivate my ups , shebecame dauntless
As if a lady trekker is heading the whole troop in dense jungle so as she
Whose kind words of appreciation demolishes my intense torment ,
When I am with her I falling in love over again as hereyes sparkle like stars
Where she was a sole climber and I was a carabineer packed with ropes

From being a simple friend to a girlfriend , she knows the real me,
From accepting who I am ,to believing in me fetching my dreams
She beholds me in every circumstance , leading meto locate myself
Holding her hands, kissing her forehead seems a bit conventional,
Where my heart just throbs for her inclusive presence around me
As the one who loves me the most Deserve the perpetual love from me.

47. THE LOVED ONE

If I thought for just one moment that this would be my last breath
I would tell you , I love you forever , even beyond death ,
If I thought for just one moment that your face would be last I see
I would stare you million times , before sleeping todeath ,
I have a feeling that I can't comprehend in my deepest thoughts
As you are more than a friend to me,
Where the mighty breeze thrashed the mountaineers unknowingly
You too came unknowingly pulling me towards you every now and then
I saw a dark cloud in the sky wandering lonely , but the silver line in it
Manifested the silver necklace I gave you , feeling a divine aroma,
With a sweet voice , I saw a luminous sunbeam shading a part of it
But your magical eyes stung in my heart with an abundant smile
When the day is about to get culminated , I remind you

Where my mind just hunts you , cherishing the incidents
We don't always agree on things , sometimes we even fight
Anytime can I return under your wings , we will set things right
But when you leave , let me know , my heart will you keep you close
Little do you know , how I am feeling , when you fall asleep .

48. MEDIOCRE SOCIETY

Living in a mediocre society isn't convenient for the grown up youths
Where the customised standards , checks growth of youths residing,
Where youths pursuing engineering is alike getting jobless whole life,
But the one who listens to the unethical norms of relatives is sagacious
As the Ilyushin needs to change its direction whenweather shatter its path
So as her Sanskar which don't lie in her jeans, rather persists in her genes
Where girls wearing shorts, is an offensive crime as per traditions
Where boys having spike and beards ,defines how unemployed they are,
As the biased society doesn't hope for a modern change , gets stocked
To the old ethnic laws , framed by grandparents, where having a girl,

Is no less a crime for a mother, who gets tortured , if she refuses dowry
Still the brutal actions gets upraised as the manipulated lad promotes it
Bearing all these frustrations, youths have an unique sense of ignorance
From least bothering dumb comments of relatives to that of employees
They prioritise self respect first , neglecting what others speak of them,
Where a man full of valorous dreams, prefers a life partner of his choice
Where a lady, committed to service, chooses a man, same as her level
As the young lady who controls a home , doesn't seek anyone's permit.

49. BOOTS AND CRAMPONS

From the freezing waves of Kanchanjunga to tip of Mt Everest
From the miniature effort to whole team effort , its dauntless
Showcasing a aristocracy in field, dominating the land by tracks
When the courage is above the efficiency of surroundings
As the cruise ship is about to tear the water folds , soas the team
Where the eternal boots and crampons are ready to get a makeable feat
When the troop was in tensed situation , the song Kutuma Kutum eased it
When the whole troop was about to conquer the summit , one voice emerged
The voice of consistency , the voice of team work , the voice of Indian members
As the trekking shoe is incomplete without the quechua soals , so are the members

Whose inherited spirit makes them a brave lad , who are competent to summit
As the work is to be done , where the chilled waves splashes their wildcraft rucksacks
Bearing the fierce low oxygen level , this troop is all set for the dream
A dream which united them all , a dream which made them move overnight
As a mountaineer is not complete without the tents and the cylinder's
So is the whole team , whose every deed is stored as a memorabilia
Where the drop of sweat dominates the drop of tears ,
Where the group smile Dominated the personal solitude
As we are one , united under a single banner of hope , as we are one of a kind .

50. BOYCOTT DOWRY

Tears in dinner plate eyes , pain in shoulders, workload in mind
Still the demotivated soul gets some motivation , recalling struggle
Where her cruel mother in law beat her with dusty slippers ,
Where her dumb father in law , least bothered visualising this
As her husband is demanding dowry in form of jewellery and cash
Regardless of the emotions she bears , he tortures her every single day.
When the father sold all his lands, just to give her inhands of a butcher
Who idolises bikes more than that of a mother taking care of her child
Where the dowry demand is extravagant , when she's handicapped
But the hope still generates in her mind , of getting a nurtured life

Like the groom processions are incomplete without a kingfisher shot
So does the marriage is not considered sacred unless dowry.
Thrashing her with belt ,barking at her like stray dogs , using slangs
Forcefully making her drink cheap alcohol , beating her like prisoner
Reminds her of her home , and she curses her dad for this lethal action
As the house turns home with the wellness of daughter in law residing
With none having the authority to control a girl from a different father
Rich or poor doesn't bother, process of dowry needs to be doomed.

51. ALONE

From bearing the gruelling heat waves to resisting cold breezes
From cherishing the ups to controlling the sole self in downs,
I don't need anyone's favour , I just need myself , alone
Where my mind toss optimum optimism wrapped with solitude
Forming a generous coordination with my sole heart , full of emotions
As the one who is fond of crossing hurdles , won't care the ramblers
My smile hide my tears,and its been the same for long years
I seem so happy, all the time, but sadly many things goes wrong,
No one knows what my inner self wishes they just experience my agony
Somehow I manage to smile, But do you know it's fake ,
I am dying inside, wishing they could feel my frustrations
I know the truth,but its locked inside me and now its tearing me apart
Where the success was about to touch the stars , a moment arrived

Where the depression tried to suffocate me , every now and then
But the least bothering mental thoughts were fearless to face it , dust from idols
As the sprinkling water from a jet spray vanishes the
So am I, whose clear way of sophistication is sufficient to demolish fear.

52. LABOUR DAY

Pain in dinner plate eyes ,thirst in throat, isn't enough
To portray a labourer code of conduct in open fields ,
Where immense urge for food is shattered by his owner
And the quintessence is least bothered to a larger extent
Where the self soul just waits for the sun to shed ,
To earn a sum, to feed and a plate of meal , to succeed
Firm grips, strong arms , fearless attitude defeats the crisis
Where the lonely heart just remember his family now and then,
As the dense hill doesn't get its essence without the shade of trees
So does his family, which gets a blow when they hear his faint situation
Strict in action , easy in passion his humble mind isn't interrogative
Where his hand movements carves the building blocks of the project
Silly as it seems, rough as it feels, kills their hours of fearless dreams
Where the small wage of a humble labourer depicts the entire scene

Domination from the owners doesn't snap their secularist approach
Where ,struggle for a living is shared by the brothers of same blood
As the one who sculpt others home , himself gets neglected by the egocentric society.

53. DRUG ADDICT

I robbed my family , misdirected my kids, tormented many
I raped my own potential thoughts, full of undaunted visions,
Where my ideas were alike river flows, which hasno partitions
Where I leaded a troop full of endeavour, don't regard me now,
Its true , but I can't get rid of these easily ,which ruins my entity
The lure of big money, for those drug dealers jerks is misdeed,
The marshal crimes, with their network reach, sucks like a leech
As you can't guess depth of a cavernous forest, by observing
So as I ,whose way of formal existence seems non identical,
I might look customary but it has a very deep meaning to it
Sucked like a vacuum, I held my fear and all sensations together
Brimming up with anger , I don't need anyone near my milieu
Shaking and trembling is what I feel , every split second

Purging my thoughts is how I heal, facing jinxed nights ,
Feelings of emptiness that everyone gets least bothered,
Disappointed climbs the walls inside my chest as I ponder
Over it , as my crime can be forgiven, but never be
forgotten.

54. RAINDROPS KEEP FALLIN'

Busy in assignment, I decided to take a break , randome top
Slowly and slowly the dumb weather got adorned with clouds
Where ,even the small rain droplets is no less my flurry drops,
And the chilled weather is more intimate than climate changer
Straight away the fervour instructed my mind to devise a poem,
Based on tranquil, freezing, faint raining, stormy grey weather
Rain Droplets clatters the roof, alike the tramp of hoofs
Where a little girl extends her palm to accumulate the drops,
Where the gleaming forest transforms into murky woodlands.
Reviewing the weather, my amorous mind, glimpsed her
Zephyr Winds coerce her pleasing hairs to swing to and fro

Where her eyes embellished with kajal, pilfer the entire show,
And her footing on the rooftop with a cup of tea ,commands it
But entity gets a pause, when her mother discern this interplay
Tongue tied in action, busy in conversation, she gets tethered,
Requite love gets enriched as rain, utters to love significant other.

55. ALL THESE DISTURBED NIGHTS

Everyone gets least bothered, when I portion my inner torment
From cigarette addiction to terminating it in porn compulsion,
No one cares ,but they too gets victimised with these liege lords
Everyone keeps idiosyncratic, but curse themselvesevery day,
As there are two or three to acknowledge, others to vilify this
Lack of partisan amplify my mental vexation leading to jones .
This honcho Increases my negative fascination to afar extent
I hoodoo myself after gobbling this venom, still I can't cease,
It urges me every now and then, whenever I am unchaperoned
May it be smoking or masturbation, it chomps my brain up,

Under peer pressure, the tongue tied mind directs to intuit it
Slowly, I feel the toxic vibes to dispatch these on a regimen.
Reposing on these doodah, I write off others, I loose my label
Good for mind, anguish for build, I discern, still imbibes it,
Ignoring my kinsman's for sake of this, is not pardonable
As the one doting me, don't covet to spot me guzzling this,
Where I am just a flimsy shore trying to avert the seiche
Somehow musters underpin, and conceal soul self with plan.

56. GENDER PREJUDICE

I looked at the billabong adams ale with a suspicious lurk
Because of how it seemed to be ceaseless and stays incessant
For the personal objective of whomever , where thesociety
Gets lively contemplative of differentiating male and female,
Where the abstraction of homemaking gets labour saving
Least bothering their education and demolishing their passion.
As the murky jungle misprizes without lofty trees and terrains
So as the society, denigrates where females are thrown over,
If only a male is authorised to clutch intrinsic decisions of family
Female role gets a domination in mediocre egocentric coterie,
If a bodach stays abide of emotional lachrymose jiffy of ménage
Why he maltreats a female snubbing his own perilous virtues.

Lets unite and stay polished by clinching their genuine needs
Doting them and fortifying them from prevailing gender bigotry
Preventing them from wild torment to the argots they discerns
From mentoring them in teens to bracing them ingrownups,
I won't utter daughters are super tranquil, or they breathe fire
Presence of a female can just be felt, all over creation of entity.

57. STRUGGLING ARTIST

Manifesting the dexterity to burgesses is alike pogonotrophy
Where there is guaranteed plausibility of cold shouldering,
Considering a few, who wassail themselves with competence
The bent which needs no inception ,still gets tumbledown,
Where the arm twisting act of society pesters him to abandon
And look for a job demolishing his agog and potent attachment.
When he quelled a phase of melancholy, this art succoured him
To subjugate his despondency easing his way of visualisation,
As the essence of a murky forest demeans without lanky trees
So as an artist who gets derailed, when someone spurns his art,
Least bothering the junctures and endeavours he lodges daily

Whimpering everyday to convoying some fine alterations in art.
Where the infirm minded were about to depress, he kindled
As a girl isn't accepted as a bride unless she provides dowry
So as an artist who is considered prodigal unless heis employed
Instead of lambasting them amplify your bankroll and cheering
To spawn talents which get showcased in world with vainglory.

58. TRACING A PATH THROUGH THE WOODS

Often labelled as ma, deadens wrath of many stray vagabonds
Who hounds psychic seclusion deep inside murky cordillera,
Discovering novel berm and fresh credence to reach destination
Which gets brimmed by the local trust worthiness of handling,
Instead of discerning the way and accepting the damp squib
Enlighten us how to suffer ache to witness the panorama.
When I get stuck in a frame of exuberance it challenges to brow
When I am utmost melancholic, it lashes an endeavour in me,
As the veridical kernel of waterfall fades away without water

So as, nomads whose ardour gets incomplete without forest,
Whose vehemence desperately hunt's flat instead of carouse
And ambience blessed with donah invigorate the whereabouts.
Blessed with vision youth often ignores the native side of forest
Gets spendthrift on thingummy which are repugnant to nature,
Where few hombre are often abandoned skewering the forest
But brobdingnagian trees, sibilating snakes, perilous bulwark,
Don't discriminates anyone entering the forest in dawn or dusk
As the one who don't fear, stay proto, forest welcomes him.

59. PHOTOGRAPHY - A PERPETUAL LOVE

Keeking through the Lilliputian hole ensnaring the vehemence
Holding it in a indefectible modulus operandi deriving attention
Discerning the belle through the image demolishesall dickers,
As the wanderer who gets adrift, when he invades the wilds
So as a photographer, who gets lost when he wins a camera
Incarcerating the english rose, manoeuvring all the colanders.
Doltish as it cognized by many takes hours of insomniac jiffy
When manus were about to give up and orb were excruciating,
And the dew drops engulfed the lens of the nonpareil camera
When vicinal were bustling brickbating citing him as a prodigal,
When fidus achates were busy besmirching his devotedness ,

He is having ones hand full discovering every pathcapturing it.
When there was hardly anyone to acknowledge my dexterity
I rubbernecked my clicked delineations and questioned myself,
Is it verily valuation dude, he gets a stalwart reply from figurine
This is not to beguile others, this is paragon your celebutante,
A stand which needs no dogma to illustrating it as idyllic
Biding abroad from all wheeling's and dealings to laze serenely.

60. DREAM OF AN OLYMPIC MEDAL

Years of dedicated execution gets heighten when they hear it
The news of conduction of quadrilinnial blest Olympic games
Contenders from far and wide join to manifest themselves
To usher lustre to country earning a medal ameliorating tally
As the hefty Adams ale lashes the shore raveging viaduct
So as an athlete, who gambols all domestic barriers to get it.
Separated by length, United by vision, abases discrimination
Glows the flame with a yearn of eudemonia and willingness
A scorching fire is enough to revamp their mental toughness
With a print of country and ménage to inflame their dreams
Providing an impetus to supervise the ground in the darkness

Everyone get in tears, when the national pennon is unveiled
Everyone senses goosebumps, when their anthem in played
Each county triumphs an emotion when they overts a medal
A medal that delineate hard work and ache in these all years
An athlete who corroborates he could defy brawl situations
To be the inspiration to billions and to preserve the proverb
To be together being faster, higher and immense stalwart.

61. EMOTIONS OF A FUNERAL CARETAKER

Envisaging the corpse adorned with floret and getting blazed
Where his son or lad yield fire to funeral pyre withdry stalks,
As such the Quintessence of body, wanes away creating a void
When all and sundry aegis his family, he conjectures about him,
He reckons it tacitly, when he discerns how the hombre was .
The caretaker questions self incessantly, did he didthe same ?
When his mother was impotent to work and he dilapidated it,
And he sensed his mother was an angel and she was arrayed
Adorned With floweret in her death bed and resting unworried,

As everyone abandon a painting, until it gets second to none
So as the presence of a person gets recognition after death,
Demeanouring all the vehemence with a wonted face trails him
Thwacking tears afore ménage to invigorate their fervours
Where he gets dilapidated diurnal by the mediocre mankind,
When there is necessitate of families they ask him for pyre
Pensiving him a jobless won't perturb as he catnaps with souls
Beholding the circs he is primed for the emotional favour.

62. INDEPENDENCE DAY

Personages gets soul stirred when they reach venerate red fort
Where the anecdote of venturesome fighters get showcased,
Bearing the dependability of country till the end of last puffs
Discrete endures goose shivers accompanied with appal zephyr
Head is held lofty with brimming hardihood and self pinpointing
Dinner plate eyes hunting pole where the flag is rejiged firmly,
Kicking ones hills for the flag to get outspread and show laicism.
Chronicles from our grandfathers, brave action from our fathers
Seems belligerent, from military stories to quotidian nationals,
From the gutsy role of Birsa Munda to bravery of Bhagat Singh
Prodigious people makes places powerful being a cut above

As lion doesn't prove anyone re his presence in murky forest,
So as India ,doesn't need any media to showcase itspopularity
When our tricolour gets unfurled and quivers withthe gale ,
When the passionate anthem is frolicked in the backdrop
It pizzazzes me to think of 139 crores Indian citizens residing
Staying amalgamated, bringing well being to grassroot natives,
As above all the religions there's a tricolour flag sheltering us
Safeguarding his countrymen from circadian manipulations.

63. LIFE IS SO UNPREDICTABLE

When I was taking a fathomless sleep in my expanse
When the timekeeper bashed noon, cold zephyr thrashed me
Suddenly, I recalled my old school friend who left uslately,
With a refulgent smile in his face and lying imperturbably
With the body adorned with attire and lucid orangeflowers,
Bidding adieu with reducing plausibility of returning back
All of a sudden my mind discerned his attendance inour school
Where he was a taciturn humourist trying to make others laugh
When least bothered by some, he started rekindling sole self
He was time poor with his incessant passion defying solitude
As the forest remains tongue tied when the greenery fades ,
So as our batch, which became voiceless when he left us.
The day I saw your fading eyesight and sleeping anxiety free

I realised life is so unpredictable and its something to esteem,
To fund some time in friendship as when a batch looses own
Identity, getting despondent with the sole memory of the dead.

64. RICH CULTURAL HERITAGE

Often labelled as mother seems commodious for many natives
When the opulent cultural heritage is unveiled as fountainhead
Lavishing the quintessence it bears enriching it's divergence,
Encouraging the youngsters to discern it's circadian existence
As a person is considered illiterate if he isn't using social media,
So as a village which is considered unworthy without culture.
Witnessing the lack of curiosity for culture amongthe youths
Indian government made an incessant quest to ameliorate it,
Starting from the regional tourism to centralizing regional artist
Escalating the specifications of Indians with culture abroad

When a gentleman and a noble woman confess the same taste,
Intensifying their relationship surging the diversity farther.
When the euphonious music accompanied by dhol nishan
Played by our brothers adorned with minted cultural attire,
Brandishing their long hairs to and fro and thwacking drums
Softens the diurnal tightness magnifying it's companionship
As Indian citizens get goosebumps when national flag is atop,
So as civilians, gets emotional when others esteem their culture.

65. STRENGTHEN THE LITERACY SKILLS

Ameliorating the level of education annually seems truculent
Where tutees of diverse backdrop fetch worthy knowledge
Quotidian man takes oath achieving sophisticated literacy,
Imparting education demolishing the narrow domestic walls
As the quintessence of river dims when flowing water dries up,
So as a country gets tongue tied when its literacy rate scorches.
Days when the mediocres intercepted the faultless to pursue
Got bullwhipped by the level of proficiency they perceived
When mentors upraised his sea change upholding virtues,
He began his voyage enduring catastrophe in every juncture
As the who stay resilient on weak taunts, receiving education,

Will bide insouciant when his drive his lambo with two seats,
Feed your kids with savoir faire ram shackling distinct grades
Teach them to hunt the perfection neglecting serious rivalries
Master them to lead their own avenue deserting arguments,
Guide them to abandon the bias between studies and sports
As a joker knowingly plays a dumb role masteringeverything,
So as a literate person, well educated to play the dumb role.

66. VALUE THE SPORTSMANSHIP

Enduring contingencies being defiant to combat any setback
As wealth of person debases when family members can't adore
So as the essence of sports abases when fans attendance lessen
Their guiltless souls cripple when players least bothers them
The motionless mind condemns the athletes for this behaviors
Waiting desperately for hours in and out the country for signs
Seems silly for mediocres attaining a specific placein emotions
Persuading to execute regime tirelessly with a hope of victory
Following the path traced by their respective icons with belief
From death valley to la ultra every trails scrooch down to them

Whose undismayed idea to run a extra mile adorns the scene
Least bothering the felicity enduring the soles of Nike Air Zoom
With awkwardness in each steps hunting all with abundance
Bidding adieu to his family members with a whimpering face
As bounded motivators matter a lot for him making a difference
Life takes a turn when event pickers gets manipulated all over .
A mindset that differentiates them from mediocre civilians
As legends follows the path opposite of dumb driven cattles
So as the runners who prefers to be a cut above ordinary.

67. FRONTLINE WORKERS

Puerile as it seems to homespuns kills hours of stalwart dreams
Where a despondent consort anticipates his helpmate advent,
Where a abandoned brat behests time least bothering doodah
As the one who took troth to serve the country withfortitude,
Can't neglect this duty when she sings to him in hour of need
Disdaining the fact, when others give a contention to him daily.
When country was prospering, lawmakers clenchedbouquet
When county was debasing taciturnly workers are condemned,
Pelted stones, dangled and persecuted if any abysmal happens
Scrutinizing the fact that country don't own good impedimenta,

Gets manipulated, if frontier workers are steered by politicos
As the billabong adams ale enters the terrains and flows away,
So as a politico who enters every jiffy and takes their allowance.
We must discern the gospel, they too have a ménage to feed
Who lodges away from home, enshrouding the psychic warmth
Still braces a bête noire, catcalling himself when no one is near
Exacerbating caseloads, down in dumps public opprobrium
Pouring scorn on laws now and then, still works perseveringly.

68. ONE SIDED LOVE

Peeping around corner of your classroom with a taciturn look
Waiting desperately at the corner of veranda to espy dearest,
Entering your class daily with no purpose to catch a sight of you
Engaging friends to talk to you and forge me a mutual friend,
Seems a bit unhandy, but I did it, just to sign I was loving you
I loved you so much, but I was not prepared to confess it to you
Best friends fortified me to confess my love but I was timorous
Which made me herculean every juncture I tried to grab you,
Made many sacrifices to manifest my love, which seems stupid
When you refused me, discerning I cold shouldered best friends
As the waves of sea returns it's origin after hitting manky shore

So as my psyche, which was set to gain it's idiosyncratic pavilion
Babbling to the dusky darkness to walk away with ardour
Meandering like a tight lipped driven cattle with bugger all,
Seems perplexing but my devil may care mind was able to fix it
I loved you but I didn't force you to proliferate the intimacy,
As the thrashing rain droplets besmears the wizening forest
So was I, whose despondent soul was primed to repel refusals.

69. PRAMOD BHAGAT: PARA BADMINTON PRODIGY

My eyes filled with tears when I deciphered his memoir
When a senile inborn disorder semi deadened his left leg
The unbroken situation swapped when he lost his father,
Enduring the torment reckoning the struggling days in Atabira
As the lion remains king of the jungle least bothering mediocres
So was he who spurned the spent juncture with visionary goals,
Starting his odyssey with friends brace ending it inIndian jersey
Accolades carries no weight as he is busy inspiring the youth
As the fighter pilot takeoffs the jet discerning the bad weather,
So as the players who are ready to fly with cabinet reinforce.

When India was time poor rekindling their efficient athletes
Para athletes paved the scuffling way to prove their existence,
From being differently abled to attesting a ray of hope in tally,
Seems stout hearted, as games doesn't ratify domestic walls
Then who gave the sovereignty to pedestrians to vilify them.

70. DESI CHAI TAPRI

Ventilating the heart rending jiffy seems alike a piece of cake
When my brothers put together their tricky plans to decipher it
With Masala Chai, Gold Flake in left and Instagram in right hand
Using some extravagant Slangs as kind words of appreciation
As the forest trees looses greenery when rain fails to summon,
So as I, who gets in remoteness when brothers failsto haunt.
Inspiriting my ups and enduring my downs demolishes agony
When the ebullient phases are summoned with Cigarette pack
With packets full of Pan Bahar and flask full of Limon Chai,
As the Tapri is assembled by gym freaks and workout masters
Favoring less sugar chai made without espresso machine,
As the hand exertion of the Daa replenishes acute emotions

Splitting the bill among brothers sucking the squeaky clean
Where he is made to pay the exorbitant amount of invoice
Diverging the Sting and Happydent seems we are uncultured,
Packed with proficiency, sharing their manoeuver with ease
As a girl isn't considered married if she doesn't use vermilion,
So as our bond, which is inefficacious if we don't share lighters.

71. A SCENE AT RAILWAY STATION

Location that enables travellers abandoning the domestic walls
Allowing everyone to commence their beyond price journey
Enduring his firm sentiments, twinkling on his departure
Reviewing tickets all of a sudden casting aside manipulations
As the defiant skills serves as a stout pillar for affluent persons
So as the station succours as a sentimental pillar fortravellers
Family bidding adieu when he departs his hometown with grin
When mother whimpers behind the doors, father discerning it
Perceiving the success story of his kid he gets over sentimental
The undaunted story compelling hometown dwellers to adorn
Railway station with florets kicking off the series of enjoyment

Focusing the split second appointing unyielding troops for sure
Announcing the arrivals and departures of every junctures
Working tirelessly to make the scintillating journey agreeable
As the shimmering light from a distance alerts the advent,
So as the obstreperous band played portrays a successful story.

72. BRAND ENDORSMENT

From portable mass produce to substantial business in locale
Everybody using this principle to sale their requisite possessions
Meandering public dwelling places to publicize their goods
With a caramel coated illustrations dominating the market
As faultless person like Indian athletes get trappedin this
So as the mediocre society who endorse this itemsfor money.
Ramshackling the content of item and its detrimental sequel
Companies adorned with funds wins the certitudeto capture
Taking a huge steer in their rivalry upscaling its brand workers
Providing huge scale employment for the civilians seems feisty
Succouring them with various rewards encouraging their living

Earning a quotidian bread wandering seems user convenient
Being under no command who box someone's ears every day
As the lawmakers uses compassionate words before election,
So as the brand salesman who speaks feebly before they vend.

73.
ENVIRONMENTAL CONCERNS

Initiating the concern with wildfire to incessant adulteration
These delicate controversies needs no introduction to citizens
Inhabiting in its base chasing their dreams with proficiency
Using its artefacts for individual use discarding everywhere
As a country abases with the depleting law enforcement
So as our environment which abases with increasing impurities
The whimpering wild animals, the strained country dwellers
Condemning themselves as these predicament devours them
Aggregating their family members in amplifying the death toll
No one perceives the crisis unless it barricades the prosperity

Getting throttled with the gloom ridden perspectives of items
Attenuating ozone layer augmenting profound temperature
Paving a way for natural misfortunes to grasp their pavilion
Taking revenge of erroneous conducts people showers deftly
As the media channels exposes the family matters in the public,
So as the summit reports reveals depth of issue disdaining it.

74. EXPLORING THE ABANDONED HUT

Smooching soil and kicking off the expedition towards jungle
Schlepping some refreshments accompanied by adams ale
Scrutinizing the murky split seconds conceiving the route
A cut above the imprinted footprints covered with dry leaves
As bikers least bothers the unpredicted crisis discerning scenery
So was our team halting to glance scenery after a resilient climb
Concocting route with obstructions seems awkward for cattles
Following the trekking track alongside the itsy bitsy waterfall
Discovering manifold proficiency to endure the stiff experience
Kicking around incidents of life bridging and smiling placidly
All of a sudden friends descries a small imperceptible hut

The adorned hut was an ideal residence for forest inhabitants
Assassinating wild animals using their body parts to its fullest
Enabling us to discern adoring the way of nonsedentary lifestyle
Taking a furlough from our hectic schedule tapping to top notch
Sensing sentiments of friends during their triumph and defeat
As the grown ups gets addictive to beer when they guzzles a nip,
So as the ramblers who gets addictive to landscape beholding it.

75. FADING OF MEDITATION AND SPRITUALITY

Ardour combats rejuvenation taking a day off perceiving it
When our exhausted framework suspects the chilled breezes
Eyeball glimpsing the knockouts of the begrimed environment
Eardrums tuning to the gratifying reverberations abundantly
As athletes undergrounds themselves before the final match
So as our soul which demands a solitude phase forrefinement.
Junctures when my course mates lodged apart making me lone
Introspecting the situation imperturbably with a combating soul
Congested with manifold resources diverting my sentiments
Least bothering the proposition my mind stalks perfection
Bewildering mind connecting it to individual proceedings

Detaching the luxurious living leading a contemplative life
As unlettered grownups chases the trend without discerning it,
So as the waged employees who least bothers acknowledging.

76. FARMERS PROTEST

Withstanding the scorching heat waves round the clock
Combating the crop failure when monsoon fails to roll in
Jinxing self unfailingly and departing for work when sun arises
Seems user friendly for the mediocres who enjoy the alleviation
As a bear get spotted in roadways when forest are disfigured,
So as the farmers who summons highways when they are hurt.
None cares the suicide rate graph of farmers discerning all
The irrelevant ideologies of water division leading to drought,
When the media channels trends dumb ministerial ideologies
Visualising the demise of family members he gets ferocious
Venturing to hunt the lawmen, media flaunts him as a terrorist
As the one who works in fields gets no perquisite underpin,

The anxious farmer talk to his soulmate every night with care
Visioning to provide education to his kids seems hair brained
When the manipulated lawmakers thrashes farmers with plans
The schemes requiring remunerations behind bars for approval
As the dense jungles gets fucked up when tourists invades them,
So as the farmers who gets exploited feeding Indian citizens.

77. FIGHTING THE VIOLENCE

Augmenting molestation, sexual assault in every towns
Constrains educated girls to stay at their homes with angst
Country where ill males scrutinizes their body parts before
Leading it to a greater abundance to showcase their inner parts
As the country gets fucked up when lawmakers gets ignoramus,
So as the society gets worthless with people of this mentality.
Life takes abrupt turns when her soulmate silently auctions her
Conceding others to use her to an extent that provide hard cash
Ramshackling her family crisis and frustration she comprehends
She inculpates herself when she discerns violence case in media
Where an faultless girl is being assaulted and brutally raped

Discerning public take no actions as they don't feel personal
Father sending his bold girl to mega polis to make advancement
Nobody discerns her way of life perturbating to communicate
As the despondent news forebodes her soul every second
Leading to a psychic disappointment perceiving astand point
As a overnight mission gets accomplished when troops support,
So as the country prospers when strong laws and police support.

78. FLOODED VILLAGE

Taking a day off from my frenetic schedule seemed eccentric
Removing the mucky cloth from my Enfield with dexterity,
Hitching a bag full of pourboire to apportion among needful
Commencing the journey least bothering the heavy downpour
I handpicked the mud caked road linking that adorned village
Discerning the situation promptly my emotion ramshackled
The adorned village is utterly submerged under floodwater
Roads turning to canals, plough land transforming to pond
Family members shedding innocent tears screaming for help
As the dearth medical facilities escalates throbbing death
Where the survival of a guiltless individual is not a dicky bird

Thronged with hunger and water borne lurgy kills them tacitly
As the troops gets frustrated when office bearers malfunctions,
So as the villagers, gets tensed when administration acts up
Paving a subway for media engendering to socio political chaos,
Tangling the manipulated politicians to condemnthe synopsis
Using the government helicopters for day trips around the area
Resulting in a tongue tied answer during a press conference.

79. INDIAN SPORTS FAN

From reinforcing their triumphs to using vulgar in their failure
Believing in them in their thriving phase underpinning them
Possessing their banners showcasing sentiments towards them
Enduring contingencies being defiant to combat any setback
As wealth of person debases when family members can't adore
So as the essence of sports abases when fans attendance lessen
Their guiltless souls cripple when players least bothers them
The motionless mind condemns the athletes for this behaviors
Waiting desperately for hours in and out the country for signs
Seems silly for mediocres attaining a specific place in emotions

Persuading to execute regime tirelessly with a hope of victory
Following the path traced by their respective icons with belief
Adorning their rooms with their firm attainmentsand laurels
Embellishing country with decorations initiatinga new chapter
Impelling parents to abandon the persisting discrimination
One bridging educational success and other to skilful victories
As the presence of a pretty girl amplifies the way of showing off,
So as the presence of cheering fans escalates their performance.

80. INDIAN STREET VENDOR

Endorsing their commodities bruising their throat whole day
Initiating from a low pitch and ending it in a mellifluous one
Possessing variety of customised products with subsidised rates
Preferring Luna over his Hercules for ponderous commodities
As a mountaineer ascends the summit with bounded members,
So as the peddler who meanders with freaks of same genre.
Financial predicament compels him to vend these commodities
Mental rigidity impelling him to work under scintillating sun,
Grossing a daily bread to feed and dine with his family member
Lingering hungry for numerous nights seems valetudinary
Humanitarian temperament forces him to provide service,

To succour needy with an affordable rate with great abundance
Writing the whole whereabouts in paper he shed dumb tears
Combating his body torment and daily dissatisfaction with hope
Dealing with diverse people with countless remunerations
As the peeled skin of a mountaineer expounds the ache,
So as the dinner plates eyes of him narrates a story.

81. LIFE OF MONKS

Earning the godliness at such a tender age seems scintillating
Abandoning the luxurious malice for surroundings with mastery
Fabricating the focus in monasteries with a sight oflearning
The indoctrination that frames them a self stimulated person
As the Military personnel's drinks old monk after an expedition,
So as the monks who enjoy split seconds with a specific regime.
Encountering hard workouts every day while mediocres faint
Fraughting less ordinary ways of survival while others collapses
Renders a trained person mastering studies, culling weapons
When the debilitated locals fails to provide safety to citizens,
Casting aside a hope of politicos awarding them with medals

As their mental training provides a weightage to fearlessness,
Life takes turn when Indians compares them to local molesters
Sensing they are the same to those assault people for pleasure
Understanding this with ease dilapidating the complete scene
With a right intension of bringing prosperity to commoners life
As the essence of school abases when students commits crime,
So as the essence of monastery fails when monks executes sin.

82. LEFT WING EXTREMISM

Wandering around the deep jungle discerning themselves as kings
Commencing the day with ruse and closing it with bombings
Shifting their whereabouts like a shot to reroute local police,
Traversing the slit concatenating jungle and neck of the woods
As jackals don't brace the audacity to attack the wrathful lion,
So as their troops don't bear the credence to attack our vexed Jawans
Intimidating the local villagers to pick weapon against Indian soldiers
The political ideologies mortifies when a kid refuses this for a career,
Killing him relentlessly, hanging him in presence of tongue tied villagers
The disheartened mind grants to pick armour to put an end to menace

As Maoism itself don't guarantee the well appointed daily bread,
Using the upstanding as weapon against the lawmakers seems taciturn.
Educating villagers to pick work, creating employment for a daily bread
Acknowledging infants and all age groups for a societal surrounding,
Endowing fresh roadways connecting all with incumbent centres
Abandoning the manipulated lawmakers who spoils the squeaky cleans
As river water flows swiftly when barricading rocks are removed,
So as the country prospers when high admins of Maoism are confined.

83. NOTHING LASTS FOREVER

Reminiscing the events as hardly any helped when he thrived
Commencing from dawn to dusk he consoled his soul for ache
Instilling the ideology that nothing lasts forever in this society
Abandoning the besmirch other provides every singleday
As the undaunted temperament of lion makes him jungle king,
So as the dauntless orientation of a person makes him pretty.
Accomplishing the daily dozen before the town dwellers arises
Working tirelessly each step to fetch the lifeblood of body ache
Running an extra mile to improve his self forbearance with ease
Believing his self stimulating in making combating discomfort

Paving a way for faultless grownups to take a word of honor
An affirmation involving the sole self and the better half in glass
Narrating hundred story discerning the same whereabouts
He might go down with a stout heart as his accomplished works
Which remains as a remembrance for many who admired him
Connecting the incidents sole self which a writer perceives
As river water flows like the clappers enriching its happiness,
So as a writer who executes manifold works for self satisfaction.

84. OBEYING THE HEALTH PROTOCOLS

Sheathing their face with n95 masks following the protocols
Being devised by expert cognoscente medical panel of country
Paving a path for greater abundance vanquishing the crisis
Aggregating people of manifold sectors to cooperate in this
As the king takes charge of shielding his civilians from fate
So as the troops of county who works tirelessly to shield us.
Life takes a turn when manipulated politicos supports the crisis
Involving themselves in honest work eradicating this torment
Discerning the ache allocating food and necessities to needy
Urging them to join hands in this regime for a productive future

Safeguarding the country with a vision to abandoning dilemmas
Individual of cities to village no one gets least bothered by them
Frontline workers works busily ignoring their personal matters
Injecting vaccine with dexterity to millions seems within reach
As the river water flows Incessantly until its blocks itself,
So as the advancing crisis fades itself after wrecking lifestyle.

85. PROTECTION OF RIGHTS OF OLDAGE PERSONS

Entity takes an abrupt turn when their little ones betrays them
Adducing mediocre reasons relating their idiosyncratic crisis
Picking side of their manipulated wife who transmutes him
Forsaking the safe keeping which the old age group demands
As a rich ignoramus man can't level up if he is ill starred,
So as the innocent tears of a old person dismantles his luxury
Tears dribbles from their unimpeachable eyes discerns it
When his son incessantly taunts him on pocket sized demands
Daughter in law abandons her kid to inter weave with them
Confined to family hellishing to neglect it with some eventuality

Junctures where the upbringing is perceived as negative
Condemning the oldage to upraise their kid with melancholia
Haling from a town or a village plays no role with vehemence
When a old man beseeches for daily bread and shelter busily
When a old woman is impotent to manifest her real torment
Cursing her sole self every night being downhearted to survive
As the luxurious lawmakers heeds their pets more than kids,
So as the care for old age people must be paramount concern.

86. RESTING BY THE RIVER SIDE

Cross examining about the imperishable flow of river water
My brother took me for a pleasure trip to our adjacent river
Discerning the long legged grasses covering the river pavilion
Glorifying the whereabouts with cold breeze passing over
As the military jets take ups least bothering the weather
So as the river which keeps flowing despite the obstructions.
Catnapping alongside the river perceiving its holy genesis
Easing the torment of farmers when monsoon fails to summon
Involving peoples of manifold background enjoying its vista
The scenic beauty blessed with gentleness and harmful terrains
Scatter-brained as the unconfined water seems kills dwellers

When the softness is substituted with the alarming water levels
Hailing from a small town where the vogue for nature is high
Sensing the vibrance of the hustling accessible river water
Sharing our tongue tied awkward hush hush seems truculent
As when people of indistinguishable taste aggregates together
As the soldiers releases their vexation on the remote militants,
So as an individual releases his rigidity resting alongside river.

87. SCHOOL KILLS ARTISTS

Entailing persona in a skilful act is a loathsome misdemeanour
Designed by the school jurisdiction abandoning the fine arts,
Centring the ideology, forcing student being alike driven cattles
Admiring the senior batch topper with no genuine justification
As a youth is considered illiterate if he abandonedsocial media,
So as our kids, considered prodigals if they masterartistic skills.
Incarcerating students to classrooms utilising their game bout
Succouring them to decipher question least bothering solutions
Stimulating them to linger apart from artistic skills detesting it
Presuming artists as unemployed persons dwelling in this area,

Contributing sweet fanny adams in pocketing laurels to country
As legend Kohli himself approves he wasn't good at school
Life takes an abrupt turn when parents conjoins with school
Predicting the entire career of a student from a dumb report
Condemning his kids over less score ramshackling their interest
Crashing to guide faultless to permute their idiosyncratic skills
As the unskilled education tutors to be a part of stampede,
Least bothering visionary target of establishing a self empire.

88. SENTIMENTAL DETORIATION

Time poor in overawing others in this manifold community
Chasing transcendence in every juncture slaughtering emotions
When a grownup youth exhibits his exasperation persistently
Bull whipping faultless of delicate backgrounds in each domains
As the politicos cold shoulders village dwellers afterelection
So as our feigned educated youths annihilates others after use.
Procuring lavishing commodity seems convenient for prodigals
Scourging quotidian youths to recognise them as veridical fiend
Where the ailing perspectives kills apportion with an intent
A justification involving the bloodthirsty intellect greeting ache

Deducing biased convictions citing them as saga of these games
Discerning bounded knowledge manifesting them as liege lords
Compelling other to esteem his eminent qualified background
Incapacitating others for his peculiar aid neglecting the scenario
As the non formal awkwardness demolishes with a bright smile,
So as our mutual sentiments which dwindles withthe ill will.

89. SOME FRIENDSHIPS CAN BE MEASURED IN MILES

Intense irritation in toes, peeled skin of feet with chafed thighs
Drowsy mind hunting the finish line with stalwart endeavors
Engraving an unhackneyed path for youngsters to admire
Beating around the bush for an uncompromising regime
As a lion carve trails amidst the hazardous murky jungle,
So as an Ultra marathoner who carves trails in the course.
From death valley to la ultra every trails scrooch down to them
Whose undismayed idea to run a extra mile adorns the scene
Least bothering the felicity enduring the soles of Nike Air Zoom
With awkwardness in each steps hunting all with abundance

Bidding adieu to his family members with a whimpering face
As bounded motivators matter a lot for him making a difference,
Life takes a turn when event pickers gets manipulated all over
When the higher authority condemns the long distance runners
Keeping an eye on these dilemmas they run for mental peace
A mindset that differentiates them from mediocrecivilians
As legends follows the path opposite of dumb driven cattles,
So as the runners who prefers to be a cut above ordinary.

90. STRANGER IN A TRAIN COACH

Scotching my official allegiance, I took a gooey break
Adjuring a tea, moving towards the kissing train gate
Discerning the vehemence of hills and shallow streamlet,
Where the idiosyncratic rail tracks exhibited kooky smell
Out of the blue my eyes glimpsed a person inside train coach
Beseeching for money with no dithering with a sheeny smile.
Adorned with a coruscating saree with a pair of tidy bangles
With spondulicks in both hand, pummelling it continuously,
From soliciting money individually to interrogating it in troops
They retain well building standard for being stout hearted
As the blessing of a teacher is mandatory for distinctive triumph,
So as their blessings which preserves the reverence protection,

Dawdling the being in the inception to probing their walk of life
Seems out of ordinary for many but none cares the appendage
The lusty alliance that demolishes the manipulated lawmakers,
From adorning jeans inside the skirt to cajole they are bonkers
As the society couldn't progress with tapered domestic walls,
So as the county which derails with the persisting prejudice.

91. THAT EMOTIONAL DETACHMENT

Receiving this unconcluded letter from a well known confidante
Thinking back to those exuberant moments from dawn till dusk
My soul desperately seeks you far and wide amidst the jaded days
Lashing the despondence, consoling my mind to stay non complaint
As the trees of dense jungle gets lapsed when monsoon stays apart,
So as the emotions of a man gets void when the better half stays apart.
Words can't begin to cover the love and emotions she down poured
The contagious smile with crazy sense of humour makes me distracted
The over elaborating love which seems taciturn forfolks, can't discern

Cursing the sole self every night time for this uncharted detachment
This unknowledgeable society fails to realise the real endearment
Chewing over it as an abiding way for squandering time with each other
As the artworks of a doting artist makes everyone feel his sentiments,
So as this letter, portrays the discomfort she must have been through.

92. THE ADORNED TOWN GIRL

Busy in picking out clothes for my appealing friend birthday
All of a Sudden, my friends discerned a fine beauty advancing
Whose ponytail was tossing the perpetuity adorned with a bun
Embellished with kajal and pierced vivid earrings in both ears
As the lawmakers speak squishy words before the election,
So was she whose way of interaction was a soft articulation.
Comprehending the scene, she started talking to me decently
Propounding me to choose her clothes of manifoldcolours
Stimulating her confidence, ameliorating her horse sense
My emotions started tossing sky, I was powerless controlling it
With scintillating smile in face and adoring specific split seconds

Cherishing the affectionate time we were having in conjunction
Exchanging numbers wasn't a big dispense as she was soliciting
With an incandescent approval, I jumped higher sarcastically
As bikers worships their bikes seeking vehemence of nature,
So was I about to get derailed discerning her unaffected beauty.

93. THE DARK TUNNEL

Visualising the tenebrosity of the journey ill hearted faints
Ramshackling the scintillating light when it gets culminated
As the stout hearted chronicles in media don't focus the ache
Highlights the amount of waged works he does dumping pains
As the train enters the dark tunnel discerning it and winning it
So as our life, which showers radiance when darkness ceases.
Days when his faultless soul is dead on ones feet hunting talent
He thinks of his family circumstances and he gets stimulated
Budding his friends to earn ecstasy for his town seems gallantry
Hailing from a town doesn't dwindles his cultural quintessence

Wearing the ethnic dress and adorning with ceremonial wears
Reflecting smile to heighten others bearing the discomfort
Grinding hours every night doesn't bothers as dinner plate eyes
Isn't abundant to describe the thriving days everyone discerns
Starting with the financial burdens, ending it in ménage issues
Everyone stays least bothered sucking his salient time for self
As an undaunted officer enters the ground tumbling down crisis,
So as a dauntless son of a mom summons darkness with vision.

94. A HAUNTED HOUSE

Bustling our cricket session near railway colony, all of a sudden
My friend envisioned a lighted doodad with an awkward sound
The sound that called for consternation exhibiting high pitches
With a bright flash of white pinafore projecting out of the room
As the jet pilot gets agitated when he reviews a drought area,
So as the house whose introspection was no less a mystery.
Invading the haunted house with my friends with apprehension
Chewing over the haunted stories of the english horror movies
With flame in our hand introspecting the house with anxiety
Discerning the dumped pictures of person depicting chronicles

The echo which delineates the vacantness of the entrance hall
As the abandoned house illustrated the diurnal trepidation
Speaking to local police to scrutiny and evacuate us promptly
Absconding out of the abrupt screenplay for over a hour
It was time to withstand fresh surrounding air of banyan tree
As the abandoned station transforms to a home for addicts,
So was the house which was epicentre for grown drug addicts.

95. THE SCINTILLATING BHARAT RATNA

Vision in mind, dinner plate eyes with an empty wallet
Travelling miles to attain their target fortifying passion
Edifying them to venerate their skills in this veridical life,
Doting the indispensable skills they effectuate to admiring it
Leaving a course of action for the squeaky clean youth to follow
Abandoning mediocre hombre who divert them, discerning it.
Commencing creative junctures with perfection in each levels
As the sketch hanged in their rooms illustrates their notion,
The notions initiating genuine rehabilitations in Legion fields
Emboldening the skillful to finish the work with devotedness
As the train follows the track amidst the darkness in Wilderness ,

So as a brave son who follows the footprints amidst the hurdles
The president of India awarding them showcases their dexterity
The artistry achieved by working under the scorching sun daily
The hope that forces the valiant to experience the awful days
With a scintillating smile sharing the prospectus for correction
As the security of flag demands the blood of faultless soldiers,
So as our real Ratnas who glitters burning their procrastinations.

96. VILLAGE MELA

Family gathering gets an amplification when village host mela
Invigorating small scale tradesman to sell their commodities
Benefiting the inventive persons to exhibit their talents
Manifolding emotional jiffies for few days with abundance
As the craze for a regional movie in Indian theatre is very high
So as the craze of mela for faultless villagers is mettlesome.
Girls of every age get hold of colourful bangles with negotiation
Mature boys enjoy the rides of the mela event reminiscing it
Luxuriating on a corner with mouth stuffed with pan envisions
Some coquettish girls getting prepared for night gyrate shows
Blessed with eye gazing sharing smirk for justified split seconds
Seems trouble free for the grown ups to esteem very moment

With worthwhile gifts in hands to gift them as a token of love
The love which ramshackles the expense of doodah gifted
Ménage members munching food jointly and ventilating it
With a cultural vibrance emboldening the effort they present
As the whole town gets lightened when a celebritysummons,
So as the villagers who lightens up their mind witha credence.

97. WALKING WITH MY SOULMATE

Holding the hands with an unyielding grip progressing ahead
Sensing the vibrance of attachment with one another steadily
Prattling the memories, taking a trip down the memory lane
Conceiving diverse plans with an eagerness to stayside by side
As sky becomes fragmented when starts doesn't scintillates,
So was she whose occupancy was a flickering factor for me.
Enduring the dwarf circumstances with slighter awkwardness
Perceiving the situation being the stimulatory pillar for other
Chewing over the ideas and prospectus to amplify competence
Seems glamorous as we cherish the phases growing together
The juncture which least bothered the lavishing commodities

The chapter which wasn't bifurcated by these nonsense stuffs
The sensation which was glorified by the incessant compassion
The vigorous feelings which crossed different barriers of life
As the quintessence of runway increases when jet lands in it,
So as our life which gets notable when a right person summons.

98. WORKING OUT WITH MY BROTHERS

The forsaken life get eccentric when friends plans a party
Agglomerating our school batch mates adoring stuffs
Kicking around the dumb issues with a diverse mindset
All the time the tireless fervor thumps to work harder in life
As a diligent cyclist finishes his race tumbling down the beauties,
So was my ferocious soul which was ready to forsake beauty.
My soul hangs about for workout brothers to accomplish a task
Assisting me in my despondence, encouraging me in my success
Portrays them as an ballsy pillar discerning my proceedings
Acknowledging it with forbearance enduring heavy workloads,
Working assiduously for the intimate person whobelieved me

As my half commitment is enough to dishearten their sprits.
The proficient workout upskills the youth to lead with regime
The routine which involves the sole stead fastness with vision
Vision leading to an arena to stay motivated roundthe clock
Beholding situations with intense torment staying ignorant
As the golfers use the golf courts without harming the nature,
So as my muscles which works hard without harming my body.

99. THOUGHT PROCESS OF A WRITER

Beholding every situation with forbearance seems trouble free
Apprehending the cause behind every chaos with tenacity
Molds him a person less ordinary to write it in a procedure
Being tranquil all the time makes him a stalwart man all over
As the best of best dwindles when they expose their prospectus,
So as he who surprises audience with new novels adducing it.
Scrutinizing his own book with attentiveness seems intransigent
Where the self written monitoring matters a lot for his notions
From discerning a weeping mother to that of a molested girl
He superintendents to draw the base line of every anecdote
Letting others regard how an author feel when he narrates

Intersticing the gates for interested intellectuals to fetch vibes
As the incessant quest to think more and more gets abundance
Writing every day when he is basically adapted to manuscripts
Casts a person who elucidates the surrounding intimately
Making a difference in influencing the youth to stay a cut above
As the hunters gains the courage to enter the deep trenches,
So as he who gains the courage to focus on ignorant issues.

100. WHERE WORDS FAIL, MUSIC SPEAKS

Tuning to the mellifluous beats forcing self to savour the song
Discerning a sudden heartbreak, intellect acknowledges lyrics
The lyrics speaking the torment, a person is going through
Remembering the junctures overnight shedding tears alone
As the tall trees wails when monsoon fails to summon,
So as an individual severs when his working earphone seizes up.
Manifesting his bitterness talking to self being despondent
Seems imbecile to mediocres without perceiving his cramp
Broaching his educational setbacks ending it in correspondence
He conceals his discomfort sharing crisis with his soulmates
Beholding the affairs with perseverance his soul gives up
Paying attention to music gives condolences to stay a cut above
Packing his song list with emotional tracks of manifold language

Sensing the sentimental ambience narrating hefty chronicles
As the train derails when track gets manipulated by others,
So as a person who combats desolation when someone dodges.

101. THE LAST LESSON

Inscribing quite a few free verse poems discerning junctures
Seems inane for others, but my soul weeps when I recollects it
The infringement civilians endures inhabiting in this country
Pouring scorn on manipulations to assaults which never ends
As no one cares a person degree when he drives a Lamborghini,
So as the writings of a author abases when readers can't espy.
Analyzing minds of intellectual people representing the scene
Suffering people to bridge their personal deeds apprehending it
Stimulating readers to thrive a self outlook intuiting everything
Following their self promenade paving way for correspondence

Least bothering the educational grades to fetch success inlife
Adoring manifold events staying apart from psychic addictions.
Bearing conviction accomplishing their duty with satisfaction
Preparing their undaunted mind to combat procrastination
Venerating the persons who trusted them when no one else did
Outspreading emotions not restricted to narrow domestic walls
As the fresh adams ale flows incessantly neglecting diversions ,
So as an author who condemns drafts ramshackling lawmakers.

102. DON'T PROTECT WOMEN , TEACH MEN HOW TO BEHAVE

Spying the cleavages and discussing about it spontaneously
Abusing a girl indicating her bra straps and assuming the size
Lambasting a decent girl who purchases sanitary napkins
Reinforcing a bastard who exacerbates these fountainheads
As the creation of mankind isn't substantial withoutmother,
So as a society, considered mediocre, where girls aremolested.
Life takes a hurried turn when rapist are set free in the country
Strident assaulters are supported by those aristocratic politicos
Sex traffickers who brutally injures female parts for payback

Forge ahead to old sex fiends, forcing them to have intercourse
But the still country gets busy elucidating the religious disputes,
I am not really a person with diurnal guilt free frame of mind
But my heart thwacks when a father get tensed for daughter
A humble brother adorns a fierce mentality when he gets it
Instead of threatening our girls to wear shorts in public places
Upskill your Men to change his long in the tooth ideologies
As the entire breed of monkey is reckoned from their conduct,
So as those mentalities which manifests their skint upbringings.

103. FOOTBALL : A NEVER ENDING LOVE STORY

Fastening the robust shoestrings with ample convenience
Packing the weeny sack with drinks that approbate exuberance
Scrutinizing the pressure of the ball with prodigious vehemence
Seems buddy buddy to one and all who are so into this game
As a strapping relationship too stipulates mutual apprehension,
So as this game which behests consummate adherence to rule.
The junctures from chalking up goals to oozing thedivine orb
From nutmegging one to commending his hasty competence
The persistent tutelage from my companions made it fecund
When an equitable player summons to thrash our tribulations

These anecdotes of my hometown shadows me to recall it ,
Squalling with agony, the taciturn soul seeks the grassy grounds
Entity gets a breakneck turn when government least bothers it
When manifestation of dexterity to others is like pogonotrophy
Episodes when our grounds used to be hub is now a crib plot
Desolated by the domains, player ultimately paves adieu to this
As wild animals weeps when they are intentionally mutilated,
So as a player whose eyes get filled when he discerns this game.

104. I AM SO INTO YOU

Meeting you at the cafeteria with an insouciant persona
Clutching your hands and jerking you towards my arms
Canoodling your lips, gracing your pixie cut coiffure
Twinkling whilst with an alluring requite apprehension
As the murky forest gets abridged without the thick mist,
So as we, one is incomplete without the correlative affection.
Recollecting your scintillating countenance when I am taut
Prattling to you with your sycophantic words of admiration
You grappling me in your arms, smooching my forehead
Making each juncture adorable where our orb tails quietude
Commencing with unhandy plans, culminating it inmomentos
The jiffy gets a high commendation when others discern it,
Assimilating each other at their downs bracing our mutual ups
Seems cumbersome for the one who cannot discern it at first

Gets fascinated when they comprehend our benedictory story
As the cavernous forest potent its visitors get happy go lucky,
So as our alliance forces us to leastbother baseless tribulations.

105. UNEXPECTED FRIENDSHIP

Kicking off an iffy day and winding it up with a dumb perplexity
Seems cumbersome for mediocres who aren't inclined to intuit
Time poor with idiosyncratic bide engrossed in echt deference
Allures the striking with venturesome endeavors bracing it
As the jungle calls for dew drops to ameliorate its landscape,
So as our tongue tied esse prefers a companion to get perky.
Underpinning my dinkum despondence, inspiriting my walkover
Taking a sip of queer for sake of amity bespeaking intimacy
Grasping our vernacular lingo to get the hang of manifold slang
Lavishing o clock with each other to remunerating it oneself
Stimulating each other internally with an enraptured persona

Discerning the whimper to embolden her scintillating grin
,
Abandoning the melancholic past idolizing the contemporary
Scrutinizing the correlative endearment with firm apprehension
Seems inutile for confidante where day culminates with a tiff
Empowering us know about selfsame intensity of attachment
As the journey of ascending a hill starts with progressing steps,
So as our bonding which commences with jovial junctures .

106. HE WRITES.. SHE SINGS

Imprisoned in the domain of knack our sight gratifies hush
Apportioning the alike persuasion with a wish of complacency
Sanctioning our ajar commitment jingle to self appeasement
Seems cumbersome for some who can't acknowledge it
As the frondescence of jungle tunes to manifold drizzles,
So as she whose salubrious tone tie up my poetic vehemence.
The anecdotes which deserts the give and take despondence
Junctures that consolidates our requited correspondence
Least bothered by mediocres, perceived by man of his words
Meandering unchaperoned for a bona fide undying delectation
Chewing over my melancholy seems facile when she discerns
She gets exuberant when I elucidates her loopy predicaments

Sharing kindred ideologies to culminating it in her countenance
The day winds up composedly with adulation lading to ardour
As an artist mounts an art without any outer animadversion,
So as our mutual intimacy which beats for internal pleasure.

107. I GAZED AT HER AND SHE RESPONDED

Unbending for junctures in waiting hall getting knackered
My soul directed ardour to splurge the rest of time on platform
Catnapping under the charging point my eyes were dwindling
Discerning the poles apart comportment of manifold peoples.
Out of the blue my eyes squized an appealing beautiful girl
Busy in her headphones, gazing her surrounding at intervals
Her eyes were compelling, with a scintillating countenance
Her dark coloured hair bun guarded under a sheathing hoodie
And her eyes glancing the defiant whereabouts of departures
Tuning the time poor arena to a forbearing lovey dovey abode

The vague raindrops, chilled zephyrs elevated an alluring care,
All of a sudden I googled her desperately for split seconds
She acknowledged back with a stiff smile and gawker back
Sitting alongside her batting around our journey occurrences
But life gets a dolour like a shot when her train departs
As the flowing billabong adams ale proceeds discerning shores,
So as she who meets diverse strangers, twinkles and proceeds.

108. SHE DEFINES HERSELF

Adorned with a pretty soul, she manifests a scintillating grin
Blessed with a brawny souvenir, she shares nostalgic junctures
Quarrelling with her mother and loving her father persistently
Narrates her annoyance when her manic day gets culminated
As the ethos of jungle fades away, When darkness disappears,
So as she whose presence abandons my diurnal despondence.
Clutching her teddy, clasping her pillow, sleeping modestly
Deserts the useless stuffs embellishing her temperament
Handling her studies, dispensing her vital view point to others
Delineate her nature, as her servile heart yearns compassion
Sharing endless secrets with her mother and smiling silently

Reminds her of her younger self when her eyes glanced joy.
Her face portrays a sudden smile when someone discerns her
Accepting the way she is, without contrasting her to other girl
Engraves a doting memory in her heart which glows incessantly
As a father loves her daughter till he takes his last breathe,
So as she, whose heart waits for someone to love her eternally.

109. WHY IS MENSTRUATION STILL A TABOO?

Condemning the process seems fiddly, when educated invades
Schlepping a vantage point of labelling menstruation as a taboo
As if it's a misdemeanour which females suffers periodically,
When the vehemence of a squeaky clean girl is leastbothered
As the billabong Adam's ale mashes the rocks and paves its way
So as the gutsy lady who agonizes criticism and paves her way.
Hailing from a mediocre society with delicate recommendations
Appraising the cardinal virtues of a dauntless lady in the home,
Still all and sundry repudiates when females battles periods

Designating it as sisyphean happening of minimal importance
When carrying a pad for a sister or girlfriend seems convenient
Abandoning the ideologies of lacklustres who interferes daily
Speaking to her, empowering her to rejuvenate without hurdles
Apportioning the whatsits to forge her high spirited exhilaration
When her mood swinging seems trouble free for my spadework
Comprehensioning her endeavours fulfilling her requirements
As the village dwellers becomes insolent when feelings wanes,
So as she who becomes exasperated when our emotions fades.

110. THE DARK SIDE OF WAR

Busy with their own slog the civilians portion joyful junctures
All of a sudden everyone discerns a heavy sound with flashes
Promptly the muted alarm rings up audibly and expeditiously
The tongue tied media incessantly focuses the confrontation
Within a fraction of seconds the picture of city gets dismantled
The communication ceases, circumstances seems deteriorating
As the military gets exasperated, when the militancy flares up,
So as the life of civilians gets demolished when a war erupts.
A crying mother, a weeping wife, a lionhearted husband
Slowly but surely everyone sings their death song effusively
Some burnt alive, some hit by bullets, many under debris

Protecting their country from the heinous illogical invaders
Till their last breath they gainsay the contingency of war
A war which manifests useless victory executing innocents
A war that ruins every family dilapidating their subsistence
Cursing their leaders to focus less on slaughtering humanity,
As the plinth of all religions cynosures primarily onhumanity,
So as the dark side of all wars kingpins the fate of humankind.

111. MENTAL HEALTH

Procrastinating every split second with a fear of expression
Concealing pain in front of others to preserve their patience
Eyes shedding tears every night with diurnal exasperation
Consoling their squeaky clean soul to stay undisturbed
As a girl ignores the discomfort discerning her period cramps,
So as the nature of humans, who leastbothers every torment.
Life gets complicated when no one endorse their hazy vision
Lambasting them with abrupt words forbidding their interests
Cursing themselves packing their mind to abandon expectations
Cynosuring themselves cold shouldering their mediocre slant
Seems cumbersome for those who doesn't uplift their emotions

But sentiment gets hurt when someone behold that discomfort
The discomfort that forbids the facile materialistic barriers
The discomfort that eventually destroys a guilt free mind
Moulding them to a person who understands when to dump
And accept a person with humble heart being kind to them
As every river stream connects a dumb driven to his destination,
So as every problems vehemently changes your perceptions.

112. A BEWITCHING AIR HOSTESS

Engrossed in my personal editing work, I was wornout totally
All of a sudden, my ear drums were honoured with soulful voice
A voice which was soft enough to make anyone fall in love
Then came 2 to 3 beautiful ladies adorned with faint red attire
With their shaped hairs tossing eternity and eyeballs glancing
To and fro, addressing everyone with proper etiquette softly
As the flowing water streams inside jungles ameliorates it,
So as the air hostess whose presence is itself prepossessing.
Putting aside their ego and requesting everyone to tie seatbelts
With chaperoning everyone alike they are our beloved teachers
Interacting with me like a elder sister safekeeping my journey

Smiling diurnally, making me feel comfortable about their work
Of discerning proper craft politeness with an incessant quest
As a fighter pilot is considered the heart of a dauntless eagle,
So as these beautiful ladies who are alike feathers ofa eagle.

113. HAPPY DEEPAWALI

Blessed with fair vision, celebrated with a great passion
Approaches the festival of lights with all ethos of endearment
When parents wait for their kids to grace this lovely juncture
Glorifying the night with Dias, adorning themselves with sarees
Amplifying the quintessence of this mega societal festival
As the forest desertifies when raindrops ceases to bless,
So as the festival which puts life in this despondent period.
Father lighting Diaas with mother, husband with wife
Brother and sister exchanging gifts and sweets demanding love
With a compassion to discern the love for the caring ones
From bursting crackers to easing them with warm tight hug
Every action seems beautiful when we are with closed ones
To understand their emotions and reciprocate the love further
As the essence of a bond escalates when there's attachment,

So as the intimacy of families boosts up during a function.

114. FOR YOUR TOMORROW, WE GAVE OUR TODAY

Stripping my combat uniform, shifting my rifle fringe ways
Scrolling my unit's coordinate maps, reviewing it anxiously
Meandering here and there gently, smoking a goldflake
Suddenly my eyeballs got filled with tears, when I discerned it
The phase when my passion to serve before self was abundant
Subjugating the overwhelming sentiments running inside out
As a lion is pin pointed amidst the roaming dumb driven cattles,
So as our life, loving by choice and killing fiercely by profession.
When my flag wrapped coffin reaches home, accept it as pride
Console my parents, holding them close to your brave heart

Tell them how brave I was to lead a Paltan of high deterrence
Tendering my soldiers alike I am their keeper ready to comfort
Tell my wife and kids, how I used to read their letters with love
And miss them desperately, waiting for my scheduled leave day
Tell my siblings, how I earned that emblem in my camo uniform
Tell my friends,how their ardour aided me to live less ordinary
As parents put Tilak in his forehead, to ensure the safekeeping,
So are we, destined to die with the bullet written in our name.

115. A LETTER TO MY GRANDFATHER

Wrinkled Hands, twinkling face and soft spoken voice
Depicts my grandfather adorned with a white kurta
Relaxing in a chair, calling betaa in a melodious tune
To discern his virtues and letting me speak my own experiences
As emotions of a mother can be traced discerning her eyes,
So was he, whose dilated eyes portrayed the way he loved us.
Raising his kids to playing with their kids, he was cheerful
Holding us in his arms to gifting us chocolates he was happy
Respecting Dadi as if she's his mother to understanding her
Manifold aspects with patience made him a cut above ordinary
Being the one to chase the moon least bothering the stars
Looking at you, adorned with garland of flowers in death bed
Resting still, pointing your face towards the sky being carefree

With family members surrounding you dropping their tears
Bidding adieu and speaking how graceful your eternal life was
To Instilling a dream in me to be an commissioned officer for
Public help, Words will fall short to describe how much I loved you,
Daadaa As a person who leave his home smiling, never ever returns,
So was your contagious smile, which created an emotional void.

116. A TALE OF 2 TALKATIVE SOULS

Engrossed in adjusting my sleeper bed with greater indolence
My friend was ramshackled with his delayed irctc biryani affair
Before you can say knife an adorned young lady summoned
Blessed with a scintillating smile and a prepossessing face
Specs in eyes, exquisite hairs moving to and fro with breezes
Embellished with a black top, black jeans depicting perfection
Whose way of drawing my attention was out of my mind
As the quintessence of forest devalues when raingets delayed,
So as the essence of journey fades when she's notnearby.
Reciprocating our kind words of appreciation and opprobrium
The cold night seemed benevolent as she defined herself
From sharing her tongue tied junctures to cracking lame jokes

She made me feel alike I am a chapter of her romantic novel
Culminating her train journey seemed mutually meaningful
With the exchange of what's app number and apouted selfie
As a writer discerns the soul of the lady and sews up his art,
So as my heart thumped when I discerned her guiltless bond.

117. A LETTER TO MY EX

Walking on the abandoned tracks, espying my photos archives
Scrolling down the old evocations in a scrambling manner
All of a sudden my soul thumped, I could sense my moist hands
My mind plunged into the fine beauty of her that forged me
Who used to hold my hands and take me in her warm arms
Who used to Laugh and cry, sharing her despondent junctures
As the rainy season departs suddenly, exerting its vehemence,
So was she, who left me at once, embossing herself in my heart
Exploring the avenues of jungle, discerning the beauty together
Laughing at each other diurnally, reverencing mutual silence

Fighting with each other with no intentions to part ways where
Even a cup of Desi elachi chai was enough to quench our thirst
Suddenly the space changed, when I became an option for her
From frequent talks to minimal talks, she avoided me all over
But my soul was busy gladdening me to forgive her do In acts
Focusing on the beauty of exploring self least bothering crowd
As a free flowing river stream crosses and descryits own way,
So was she, who chose her path ignoring my emotional walls.

118. DISCERNING A CHEERFUL GIRL

Sweet as yummy Pede, cold as Punjabi Lassi
Hurt her once, she will break you thrice Stands
Bhangra girl with full of optimistic endeavours
Staring from getting adorned with beautiful authentic wears
To living a cheerful life genuinely less ordinary all over
As pain of a mountaineer fades, when he glances the summit view,
So as she, whose definition of happiness demolishes the solitude.
Blessed with plentiful communication skills with aservile humour
Furnished with humble soul for dealing diverse situation with ease
She stands still when someone least bothers her honest opinions
But life gets a sudden turn when she discerns the love of family
With father consoling her, brother boosting her confidence
Seems emotional when she stays far away from her family

To forge a career favouring service before self with gratitude
But her guiltless heart desperately wants a hug from father
To share her internal dilemmas without being judged by them
As a mother smiles, not letting others know, her internal battles,
So as she who wants someone to acknowledge her unsung tales.

119. A GIRL WITH A CONTAGIOUS SMILE

Busy with own work suddenly I discerned a grinning girl
Smiling openly, listening others with a great forbearance
Blessed with intelligence and a perspective to persevere
Possessing magic in her hands to prepare luscious dishes
Embellished with a great dressing sense to adorn her wardrobe
With an ability to transform unhappy junctures to jovial spirit
She's the one to teach me the true meaning of self obsession
As the tiny droplets of rain proliferates the soil fragrance,
So as she whose smile is enough to demolish despondence.
Not letting others know what she is going through every day
With a thousand unwieldy questions in her faultless mind,
Taking sip of coffee, sitting in her bed, nurturing her sole self
From managing her easy cough to dozing in chilled classroom
She's alike a cute kiddish girl with a well groomed personality

Willing to share her nostalgic junctures without getting judged
Waiting someone to listen to her endless talks and vibe as well
As conversation flows swiftly when we're with right person,
So as she, whose contagious smile is something to be preserved.

120. LIKE MOTHER - LIKE DAUGHTER

Intaking my diet coke, grabbing cheesy sandwich rigidly
Eyes wandering here and there amidst the long queue
All of a sudden my dinner plate eyes were lucky enough
To discern the bond of mother-daughter approaching steadily
Meandering sections to address their boarding passes to guards
Resting on the couch with a can of cappuccino, relishing it
As airport seems void when there's delay of incoming flights,
So was the duo, loving each others presence efficaciously.
Embellished with abstract talks sharing idiosyncratic junctures
Slowly and slowly mother ensuring her the solace she wants
Eyes filled with vehemence, missing someone unwantedly
Preciously listening to the sweet voice of the airlines anchor
Rushing towards their boarding gates with smile in their faces

Imprinting a good impression of them in my poetic anecdote
As the photographers can't deny for photos, if they observe it,
So was the scene, spellbinding me to adorn that eternal pair.

121. ABIDING LOVE OF PARENTS

Busy in taking a sound sleep under my warm tight blanket
All of a sudden my soul recollected the eternal care of parents
Commencing from upbringing me alike I am everything to them
To yielding me a firm shoulder to cry on my despondence
Bothering the least manifested unsung talks with forbearance
To engulfing oofy decency in me to behave as a gentle person
As the gentle river water flows without any interruptions,
So as the love of parents flows without any expectations.
Mother weeping silently behind the doors when I leave home
With father withstanding tears with a bright smile,hugging me
Not expressing their crude emotions they provide resolutely
Least bothering the gospel, I too cry steadily for their absence

Sitting in balcony, talking to the stars, and smiling wistfully
As an artist gets emotional when he discerns his own artworks,
So as my eyes tear up perpetually when I recall the eternal love.

122. MOTHER AND LABOUR PAIN

Monitoring the minute kicks, apprehending the wee thumping
Doctor consoling the family members to stay cool headed
With husband glancing her eyes, holding her soft hands,
Parting it out with a good luck, praying God relentlessly
Waiting in the common hall, awaiting for the optimistic call
Beyond forgery, eardrums holding back for the uneasy baby cry
As the undaunted sun rays erases the rasping winter breezes,
So was she, whose goodwill abandons the entire despondence.
All of a sudden, soul thumped when lights of OT are turned off,
Father rushing into the room, hugging his wife with solicitude
The teary eyes of both husband and wife is enoughto describe

The juncture when a crying kid is being nurtured with gauntlet
Shrugging off the gender, aggrandizing this day asspecial one
Culminating the pain of 9 months with abundant gratitude
As the nature loving persons, bows down to her inrespect,
So as the Labour pain of a mother, must not be least bothered.

123. THAT DAMN EYE CONTACT

On the go in taking a sip of cappuccino staring here and there
Before you can say knife my tired eyes got dilated with comfort
When I probably was not in my own governed private clearance
With a thumping heart and a broadly grinning face glancing
A beauty approaching, dressed in brown top and baggy jeans
Eyes adorned with the deep kajal firmly elevating her gleam
Loose hairs dancing to and fro ameliorating her firm beauty
Where she was alike the desperate princess waitingfor metro
With specs embellishing her chubby cheeks with lipstick shades
Fingers abstaining the tapping of phone screen with abundance

As the winters are unworthy when we forget enjoying Chai,
So was I whose priority was to increase the warmth of winters.
All of a Sudden I gazed her with a firm reply from her side
Without dilating our eyes sharing a bewitching moment gaily
Getting close to each other, smelling the way of benevolence
Initiating the topics staring from dumb to lighter intimate talks
Loosely twinkling, as her smile was a major ingredient to adore
Culminating the day, writing a poem based on her, contentedly.

124. DON'T LOOSE THE MOON WHILE CHASING THE STARS

Engrossed in our own personal space, assembling our own life
Trailing the self formulated holy grails with greater abundance
All of a sudden, my soul triggered to reconsider anattachment
Recollecting the squeaky clean faces who stood behind us
Without judging, without proliferating the scene with calmness
Getting rid of foreign elements who questions our self account
As the kernel of a person ameliorates when he departs quick,
So are we who leaves the purest souls who genuinely cares.
Being on the crescent top, brawling for the shrouded positions
Defeating others alike they don't have a life to sojourn happily

Crushing the emotions of someone who vehemently cared
Chasing someone who texts, when he gets bored over time
At some point forgetting the real we amidst the weak crowd
Dismantling our long in the tooth emotions for a stranger
As a successful man residing abroad has roots of his village,
So are we, who has life but have souls of those special persons.

125. CHOOSING PEACE OVER DRAMA

Strolling carelessly on the avenues, booting the small stones
Pelting some random thoughts, questioning my self worth
Grabbing a cup of kullhad chai, exhilarating the damn scenes
When she made me feel alike I am part of her for aseason
Abandoning me all of sudden, biased on her mood quivering
Surpassing the least bothered instances, I was a fool to discern
As the rain water bestows the parched land for a short period,
So was she, reached for a season and waned herself with time.
Mind bombarding assorted questions to soul, labelling him fool
An emotional fool, who easily gets driven by her smiling face
Treating him as an option, alike he was a commodity product

To use him diurnally absconding him whenever mood urges
Covering up her part alike nothing ever has happened before
With her eyes desperately avoiding a scintillating eye contact
As the bonny nature reconstructs itself to rekindle once again,
So was my soul audacious enough to safeguard own affections.

126. I'M WAY TOO GOOD AT GOODBYES

Time poor in taking a sip of turmeric latte in the cafeteria
Grasping my phone firmly, paginating the pics in Google photos
All at once there arouse a palsy-walsy voice next tome
My ears drums quavered, heart beating surged vigorously
Somehow I gathered audacity to peep backward leisurely
My pupils got dilated when I found she was the one who left
As the quintessence of a deep forest demeans whenriver dries
So was my squeaky clean vehemence, fragmented into parts.
The same vigor, the same glossy look adorned with kajal
Everything was the same, but this occasion it wasn't me
It was someone else whom she labelled as being 'just friends'
With soul questioning the mind of the assurances we made

Staying in league, holding each other in combating junctures
Counterfeiting a smile in my face to pave a heartfelt goodbye
As the tenebrosity of a hill decreases surpassing the avalanches,
So as the desolation a man dwindles by the insults he discerns.

127. MY HEART GOT SMITTEN

Busy in piling up the notes of previous misheardded classes
Swiping the delicate pages of copy, clicking random shots
All of a sudden, my eyes glanced a fine beauty approaching
Adorned with a patterned kurti, with long hairs tossing eternity
Soft spoken relishing in interaction with behavioral endeavors
With dinner plate eyes hunting to grasp the things being taught
As the moon scintillates dauntingly least botheringsun rays,
So was she scintillating least bothering the true tenebrosity.
Scattering the phase of despondence stands this Jammu girl
Rich with ventures, approbating a sphere to grasp Rajma Rice
Cold as ice, sweet as phirni, the weak scene gets emboldened
When her cool mind easily gets short tempered impetuously

Blessed with a clear vision to discern the delicates with ease
Understanding their emotions, ameliorating own proficiency
As the folks of Jammu are decisive enough combating breezes,
So as she defiant enough to combat the emotional barriers.

128. CHAPTER 2023: THE RISE OF THE FALLEN

Kissing the embellished year with a plethora of apprehension
Combating setbacks, extracting a life lesson to approach ahead
Crying desperately and consoling the squeaky clean sole self
Masking up junctures of intense despondence withan intent
Bridging new relationships, affirming the vehement intimacy
Taking care of the silliest things, ensuring comfort to others
As the mountains redefines herself after an avalanche mishap,
So are our life journey which must get renewed after breakups.
Holding her soft hands, discerning the lifeblood of life journey

When even a tight hug and a forehead kiss defines the moment
Spending the vigorous time with someone who mileages it
Acknowledges it without judging, nurturing our mental stability
Alike a mature husband supporting her wife in dumb instances
Culminating each day with a responsibility to push much harder
As the mother nature welcomes everyone with a wide smile,
So as the new year, impels everyone to forge a new version.

My Idiosyncratic Experiances

I was a bulky guy in my teens as i was unknown about the fitness . In my initial stages i was 104 kg . Bearing all frustations i started working out , everyone used to laugh at me there were some who motivated me and held my hand . Way back 2020 ,I could not even run 200 m or even could not cycle for more than 20 km, but i was damn sure the hardwork i put in will result someday, then i started with brisk walking , eventually leading to long runs , and ultimately i completed with 42.2 km or a full marathon , and my cycling addiction was as such i covered 108 km in just 5 hrs 45 min and i used to scale mountain twice a week to improve my endurance and breath control. This resulted mein loosing almost 36 kg weight .

"PAWAN HANS" : it was the name of my cycle , as i travelled 6000 km in this and he loved me in such a way that i cant get rid of it ....

I THANK MY PARENTS , FAMILY MEMBERS AND FRIENDS FOR BEARING ME .... (KINDA OUT OF THE BOX STUFFS)

***MY TIPS FOR FITNESS:**

1) A PROPER VISION , START DREAMING

2) HARDWOKING CONSISTENTLY

3) PROPER DISCIPLINE

4) BEAR BODY PAIN WITH A BRIGHT SMILE

5) WAKE YOU ASS EARLY

6) DON'T LOOSE PATIENCE

SOME OTHER HOBBIES :

-> I LOVE TO PERFORM MONOLOGUES ACTS

->I LOVE RAPPING SONGS

->I AM ALSO A MIMIC ARTIST

->I SING MULTILINGUAL SONGS

->I ALSO LOVE PERFORMING COMIC SKILLS

GET HARD GUYS , STAY APART FROM YOUR COMFORT ZONE TO ACHIEVE SOMETHING..

 # KALAMKAR KI SHOHRAT @2023.

9 798890 025159

Printed by Libri Plureos GmbH in Hamburg,
Germany